6 Full-Length FSA Grade 6 Math Practice Tests

Extra Test Prep to Help Ace the FSA Grade 6 Math Test

By

Michael Smith & Reza Nazari

6 Full-Length FSA Grade 6 Math Practice Tests

Published in the United State of America By

The Math Notion

Web: WWW.MathNotion.Com

Email: info@Mathnotion.com

About the Author

Michael Smith has been a math instructor for over a decade now. He holds a master's degree in Management. Since 2006, Michael has devoted his time to both teaching and developing exceptional math learning materials. As a Math instructor and test prep expert, Michael has worked with thousands of students. He has used the feedback of his students to develop a unique study program that can be used by students to drastically improve their math score fast and effectively.

– **SAT Math Practice Book**

– **ACT Math Practice Book**

– **GRE Math Practice Book**

– **Common Core Math Practice Book**

–**many Math Education Workbooks, Exercise Books and Study Guides**

As an experienced Math teacher, Mr. Smith employs a variety of formats to help students achieve their goals: He tutors online and in person, he teaches students in large groups, and he provides training materials and textbooks through his website and through Amazon.

You can contact Michael via email at:

info@Mathnotion.com

Prepare for the FSA Grade 6 Math test with a perfect practice book!

The surest way to practice your FSA Math test-taking skills is with simulated exams. This comprehensive practice book with 6 full length and realistic FSA Math practice tests help you measure your exam readiness, find your weak areas, and succeed on the FSA Math test. The detailed answers and explanations for each FSA Math question help you master every aspect of the FSA Math.

6 Full-length FSA Grade 6 Math Practice Tests is a prestigious resource to help you succeed on the FSA Math test. This perfect practice book features:

- Content 100% aligned with the FSA test
- Six full-length FSA Math practice tests similar to the actual test in length, format, question types, and degree of difficulty
- Detailed answers and explanations for the FSA Math practice questions
- Written by FSA Math top instructors and experts

After completing this hands-on exercise book, you will gain confidence, strong foundation, and adequate practice to succeed on the FSA Math test.

WWW.MathNotion.COM

… So Much More Online!

✓ FREE Math Lessons

✓ More Math Learning Books!

✓ Mathematics Worksheets

✓ Online Math Tutors

For a PDF Version of This Book

Please Visit WWW.MathNotion.com

Contents

FSA Math Practice Tests

Time to Test

Time to refine your skill with a practice examination

Take a REAL FSA Mathematics test to simulate the test day experience. After you've finished, score your test using the answer key.

Before You Start

- You'll need a pencil and scratch papers to take the test.

- For this practice test, don't time yourself. Spend time as much as you need.

- It's okay to guess. You won't lose any points if you're wrong.

- After you've finished the test, review the answer key to see where you went wrong.

Calculators are not permitted for FSA Tests

Good Luck!

FSA GRADE 6 MAHEMATICS REFRENCE MATERIALS

Conversions:

LENGTH	
Customary	**Metric**
1 mile (mi) = 1,760 yards (yd)	1 kilometer (km) = 1,000 meters (m)
1 yard (yd) = 3 feet (ft)	1 meter (m) = 100 centimeters (cm)
1 foot (ft) = 12 inches (in.)	1 centimeter (cm) = 10 millimeters (mm)

VOLUME AND CAPACITY	
Customary	**Metric**
1 gallon (gal) = 4 quarts (qt)	1 liter (L) = 1,000 milliliters (mL)
1 quart (qt) = 2 pints (pt.)	
1 pint (pt.) = 2 cups (c)	
1 cup (c) = 8 fluid ounces (Fl oz)	

WEIGHT AND MASS	
Customary	**Metric**
1 ton (T) = 2,000 pounds (lb.)	1 kilogram (kg) = 1,000 grams (g)
1 pound (lb.) = 16 ounces (oz)	1 gram (g) = 1,000 milligrams (mg)

Formulas:

Area	
Triangle	$A = \frac{1}{2}bh$
Rectangle or Parallelogram	$A = bh$
Trapezoid	$A = \frac{1}{2}h(b_1 + b_2)$
Volume	
Rectangular Prism	$V = Bh$

The Florida Standards Assessments

FSA Practice Test 1

Mathematics

GRADE 6

Administered Month Year

Session 1

❖ **Calculators are NOT permitted for this practice test.**

❖ **Time for Session 1: 60 Minutes**

1) If $x = -3$, which of the following equations is true?

   A. $x(4x - 1) = 35$

   B. $2(12 - x^2) = -6$

   C. $4(-2x + 4) = 42$

   D. $x(-7x - 12) = -27$

2) What is the perimeter of the following shape? (it's a right triangle)

   A. 5 cm

   B. 16 cm

   C. 24 cm

   D. 12 cm

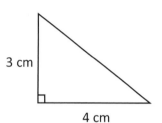

3) 60 is what percent of 25?

   A. 220 %

   B. 180 %

   C. 220 %

   D. 240 %

4) Which of the following expressions has a value of -8?

   A. $-5 + (-18 \div 3) + \frac{-6}{5} \times 5$

   B. $2 \times (-10) + (-3) \times 4$

   C. $(-2) + 14 \times 3 \div (-7)$

   D. $(-4) \times (-8) + 5$

5) 420 inches equal to …?

    A. 35 ft.

    B. 200 ft.

    C. 85 ft.

    D. 45 ft.

6) Which of the following equations is true?

    A. $0.08 = \frac{8}{10}$

    B. $\frac{30}{100} = 0.03$

    C. $3.4 = \frac{34}{10}$

    D. $\frac{35}{7} = 0.5$

7) What is the greatest common factor of 12 and 36?

    A. 12

    B. 15

    C. 24

    D. 18

8) Which list shows the integer numbers listed in order from least to greatest?

    A. $-15, -6, -3, \ 3, 8, 10$

    B. $-3, -6, -15, 3, 10, 8$

    C. $-15, -3, -6, 3, 10, 8$

    D. $-6, -15, -3, 3, 8, 10$

9) Based on the table below, which of the following expressions represents any value of f in term of its corresponding value of x?

x	1.2	1.4	2.5
$f(x)$	-2.3	-2.1	-1

A. $f(x) = x + 1\frac{5}{2}$

B. $f(x) = x - 1\frac{5}{2}$

C. $f(x) = 2x + 1\frac{5}{2}$

D. $f(x) = 2x - 1\frac{5}{2}$

10) A football team won exactly 70% of the games it played during last session. Which of the following could be the total number of games the team played last season?

A. 61

B. 50

C. 42

D. 25

11) There are 44 blue marbles and 154 red marbles. We want to place these marbles in some boxes so that there is the same number of red marbles in each box and the same number of blue marbles in each of the boxes. How many boxes do we need?

    A. 8

    B. 12

    C. 10

    D. 11

12) Car A travels 341.26 km at a given time, while car B travels 2.2 times the distance car A travels at the same time. What is the distance car B travels during that time?

    A. 650.7 km

    B. 453.5 km

    C. 341.2 km

    D. 750.8 km

13) Which of the following expressions has the greatest value?

    A. $5^3 - 4^3$

    B. $2^5 - 2^2$

    C. $3^4 - 5^2$

    D. $4^4 - 15^2$

14) The diameter of a circle is 3π. What is the area of the circle?

    A. $9\pi^2$

    B. $\dfrac{3\pi^2}{2}$

    C. $\dfrac{9\pi^3}{4}$

    D. $\dfrac{\pi^3}{4}$

15) Elise has x apples. Alvin has 45 apples, which is 20 apples less than number of apples Elise owns. If Baron has $\dfrac{1}{5}$ times as many apples as Elise has. How many apples does Baron have?

    A. 11

    B. 45

    C. 20

    D. 13

16) Find the perimeter of shape in the following figure? (all angles are right angles)

    A. 30

    B. 28

    C. 25

    D. 23

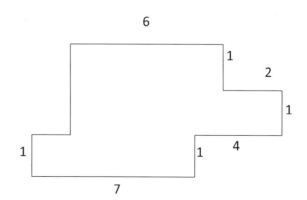

Session 2

❖ **Calculators are NOT permitted for this practice test.**

❖ **Time for Session 2: 60 Minutes**

17) In the following triangle find α.

A. 100°

B. 95°

C. 65°

D. 20°

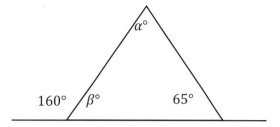

18) What is the probability of choosing a month starts with A in a year?

A. 1

B. $\frac{2}{3}$

C. $\frac{1}{2}$

D. $\frac{1}{6}$

19) $5(1.153) - 2.126 = \cdots$?

A. 1.486

B. 3.639

C. 2.369

D. 3.369

20) The perimeter of the trapezoid below is 48. What is its area?

A. 60 cm²

B. 120 cm²

C. 100 cm²

D. 88 cm²

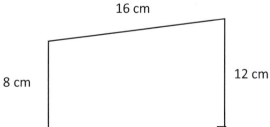

21) What are the values of mode and median in the following set of numbers?

$$1, 2, 2, 4, 4, 5, 6, 3, 1, 1, 3$$

A. Mode: 1, 2 Median: 3

B. Mode: 1, 3 Median: 2

C. Mode: 2, Median: 2

D. Mode: 1, Median: 3

22) The ratio of pens to pencils in a box is 5 to 7. If there are 144 pens and pencils in the box altogether, how many more pens should be put in the box to make the ratio of pens to pencils 1: 1?

A. 12

B. 24

C. 60

D. 84

23) Which of the following shows the numbers in increasing order?

A. $\frac{4}{2}, \frac{7}{4}, \frac{9}{12}, \frac{35}{8}$

B. $\frac{9}{12}, \frac{7}{4}, \frac{4}{2}, \frac{35}{8}$

C. $\frac{9}{12}, \frac{4}{2}, \frac{7}{4}, \frac{35}{8}$

D. $\frac{35}{8}, \frac{7}{4}, \frac{9}{12}, \frac{4}{2}$

24) If $3x - 2 = 16$, what is the value of $3x + 2$?

    A. 28

    B. 29

    C. 9

    D. 15

Types of air pollutions in 10 cities of a country

Type of Pollution	Number of Cities
A	8
B	3
C	4
D	2
E	7

1 2 3 4 5 6 7 8 9 10

25) Based on the above data, what percent of cities are in the type of pollution C, B, and E respectively?

    A. 40%, 30%, 70%

    B. 60%, 70%, 30%

    C. 30%, 40%, 60%

    D. 40%, 70%, 30%

26) How many tiles of 5 cm² is needed to cover a floor of dimension 8 cm by 25 cm?

A. 30

B. 25

C. 28

D. 40

27) A shaft rotates 360 times in 9 seconds. How many times does it rotate in 16 seconds?

A. 540

B. 640

C. 360

D. 200

28) Which of the following statement can describe the following inequality correctly?

$$\frac{x}{6} \geq 8$$

A. David put x books in 6 shelves, and each shelf had at least 8 books.

B. David placed 6 books in x shelves so that each shelf had less than 8 books.

C. David put 8 books in x shelves and each shelf had exactly 6 books.

D. David put x books in 6 shelves, and each shelf had more than 8 books

29) Removing which of the following numbers will change the average of the numbers to 7.8?

$$1, 4, 7, 13, 15, 6$$

A. 6

B. 15

C. 7

D. 12

30) If point A placed at $-\frac{16}{4}$ on a number line, which of the following points has a distance equal to 6 from point A?

A. -10

B. 2

C. -3

D. A and B

"This is the end of Practice Test 1"

The Florida Standards Assessments

FSA Practice Test 2

Mathematics

GRADE 6

Administered Month Year

Session 1

❖ **Calculators are NOT permitted for this practice test.**

❖ **Time for Session 2: 60 Minutes**

1) Martin earns \$30 an hour. Which of the following inequalities represents the amount of time Martin needs to work per day to earn at least \$250 per day?

A. $30t \geq 250$

B. $30t \leq 250$

C. $30 + t \geq 250$

D. $30 + t \leq 250$

2) What is the value of the expression $4(3x - 2y) + (4 - 5x)^2$, when $x = 1$ and $y = -2$?

A. -29

B. 31

C. 29

D. -31

3) Round $\frac{415}{9}$ to the nearest tenth.

A. 46

B. 46.3

C. 46.1

D. 46.6

4) Find the opposite of the numbers 16, 0.

A. $\frac{1}{16}, 0$

B. $-16, 1$

C. $-16, 0$

D. $-\frac{1}{16}, 0$

5) Which ordered pair describes point A that is shown below?

A. $(3, -2)$

B. $(2, -3)$

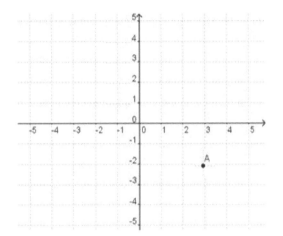

C. $(-3, 2)$

D. $(-2, -3)$

6) To produce a special concrete, for every 14 kg of cement, 2 liters of water is required. Which of the following ratios is the same as the ratio of cement to liters of water?

A. 84: 12

B. 20: 8

C. 28: 14

D. 4: 16

7) $(75 + 5) \div 16$ is equivalent to …

A. $80 \div 3.4$

B. $\dfrac{55}{16} + 5$

C. $(2 \times 2 \times 4 \times 5) \div (4 \times 4)$

D. $(2 \times 2 \times 2 \times 5) \div 4 + 4$

8) Which of the following graphs represents the following inequality?

$$-2 \le 2x - 4 < 8$$

A.

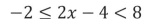

B.

C.

D.

9) The ratio of boys to girls in a school is 5:7. If there are 900 students in the school, how many boys are in the school?

A. 750

B. 435

C. 654

D. 375

10) What is the volume of a box with the following dimensions? Height = 5cm

Width = 6 cm   Length = 8 cm

A. 48 cm³

B. 40 cm³

C. 120 cm³

D. 240 cm³

11) Anita's trick–or–treat bag contains 16 pieces of chocolate, 18 suckers, 14 pieces of gum, 12 pieces of licorice. If she randomly pulls a piece of candy from her bag, what is the probability of her pulling out a piece of sucker?

A. $\frac{1}{18}$

B. $\frac{3}{10}$

C. $\frac{3}{5}$

D. $\frac{18}{18} = 1$

12) Which statement is true about all rectangles?

A: Both diagonals have equal measure.

B: All sides are congruent.

C: Both diagonals are perpendicular.

D: All the statements are true

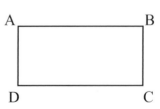

13) Which of the following lists shows the fractions in order from least to greatest?

$$\frac{3}{4}, \frac{4}{5}, \frac{11}{5}, \frac{26}{29}$$

A. $\frac{26}{29}, \frac{4}{5}, \frac{3}{4}, \frac{11}{5}$

B. $\frac{4}{5}, \frac{26}{29}, \frac{11}{5}, \frac{3}{4}$

C. $\frac{3}{4}, \frac{4}{5}, \frac{26}{29}, \frac{11}{5}$

D. $\frac{26}{29}, \frac{4}{5}, \frac{11}{5}, \frac{3}{4}$

14) Which statement about 3 multiplied by $\frac{5}{7}$ must be true?

A. The product is between 1 and 2

B. The product is greater than 3

C. The product is equal to $\frac{77}{25}$

D. The product is between 2 and 2.3

15) What is the equation of a line that passes through points (0, 5) and (4, 9)?

A. $y = x$

B. $y = x + 5$

C. $y = 2x + 5$

D. $y = 2x - 5$

Session 2

❖ **Calculators are NOT permitted for this practice test.**

❖ **Time for Session 2: 60 Minutes**

16) 115 is equal to …

    A. $-10 - (5 \times 10) + (7 \times 20)$

    B. $\left(\frac{12}{8} \times 96\right) + \left(\frac{156}{6}\right)$

    C. $\left(\left(\frac{18}{4} + \frac{30}{4}\right) \times 8\right) - \frac{13}{2} + \frac{88}{4}$

    D. $\frac{481}{6} + \frac{121}{3} + 50$

17) Mr. Jones saves $2,700 out of his monthly family income of $74,700. What fractional part of his income does Mr. Jones save?

    A. $\frac{1}{27}$

    B. $\frac{1}{24}$

    C. $\frac{3}{83}$

    D. $\frac{3}{74}$

18) If the area of the following trapezoid is equal to A, which equation represent x?

    A. $x = \frac{15}{A}$

    B. $x = \frac{A}{15}$

    C. $x = A + 15$

    D. $x = A - 15$

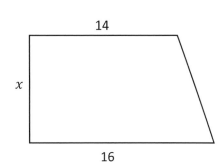

19) An integer is chosen at random from 1 to 40. Find the probability of not selecting a composite number?

A. $\frac{11}{40}$

B. $\frac{6}{15}$

C. $\frac{13}{40}$

D. $\frac{1}{3}$

20) By what factor did the number below change from first to fourth number?

$$12, 168, 2352, 32928$$

A. 14

B. 12

C. 168

D. 2352

21) Based on the table below, which expression represents any value of f in term of its corresponding value of x?

A. $f(x) = 2x - \frac{3}{10}$

B. $f(x) = x + \frac{3}{10}$

C. $f(x) = 2x + 2\frac{2}{5}$

D. $f(x) = 2x + \frac{3}{10}$

x	3.1	4.2	5.9
$f(x)$	8.6	10.8	14.2

22) Calculate the approximate area of the following circle? (the diameter is 15)

A. 98

B. 177

C. 56

D. 1130

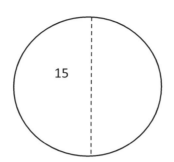

23) The following graph shows the mark of seven students in mathematics. What is the mean (average) of the marks?

A. 15

B. 14.6

C. 15

D. 1.6

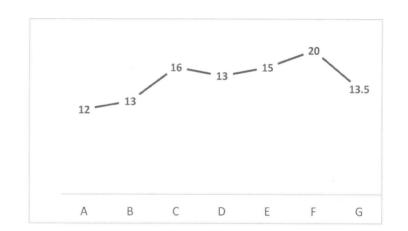

24) If the area of the following rectangular ABCD is 160, and E is the midpoint of AB, what is the area of the shaded part?

A. 50

B. 80

C. 40

D. 70

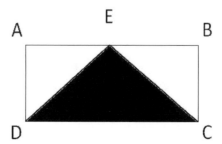

25) Which of the following statements is correct, according to the graph below?

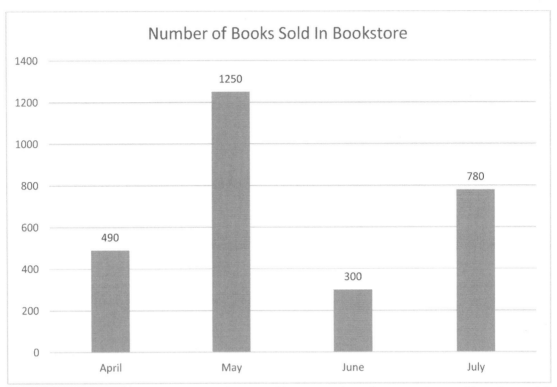

A. The number of books sold in the April was twice the number of books sold in the July.

B. The number of books sold in the July was less than half the number of books sold in the May.

C. The number of books sold in the June was more than half the number of books sold in the April.

D. The number of books sold in the July was equal to the number of books sold in April plus the number of books sold in the June

26) What is the ratio between α and β, $\left(\frac{\alpha}{\beta}\right)$ in the following shape?

A. $\frac{5}{14}$

B. $\frac{7}{11}$

C. $\frac{11}{5}$

D. $\frac{11}{5}$

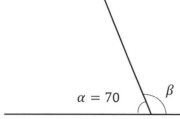

$\alpha = 70$ β

27) When point A $(-6, 4)$ is reflected over the y-axis to get the point B, what are

the coordinates of point B?

A. $(-6, -4)$

B. $(6, -4)$

C. $(6, 4)$

D. $(-6, 4)$

28) The distance between two cities is 4,389 feet. What is the distance of the two

cities in yards?

A. 1,463 yd.

B. 11,304 yd.

C. 3,826 yd.

D. 1,483 yd.

29) What is the lowest common multiple of 18 and 30?

   A. 90

   B. 40

   C. 30

   D. 45

30) A car costing \$600 is discounted 20%. Which of the following expressions can be used to find the selling price of the car?

   A. $(600)(0.4)$

   B. $600 - (600 \times 0.2)$

   C. $(600)(0.2)$

   D. $600 - (600 \times 0.8)$

"This is the end of Practice Test 2"

The Florida Standards Assessments

FSA Practice Test 3

Mathematics

GRADE 6

Administered *Month Year*

Session 1

❖ **Calculators are NOT permitted for this practice test.**

❖ **Time for Session 1: 60 Minutes**

1) If $x = -5$, which of the following equations is true?

   A. $x(3x + 9) = 45$

   B. $3(32 - x^2) = -18$

   C. $2(-5x - 10) = 55$

   D. $x(2x + 5) = 25$

2) What is the perimeter of the following shape? (it's a right triangle)

   A. 40 cm

   B. 15 cm

   C. 32 cm

   D. 30cm

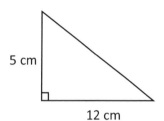

5 cm

12 cm

3) 63 is what percent of 30?

   A. 221 %

   B. 121 %

   C. 120 %

   D. 210 %

4) Which of the following expressions has a value of -11?

   A. $-8 + (-32 \div 8) + \frac{-5}{6} \times 6$

   B. $4 \times (-10) + (-6) \times 3$

   C. $(-5) + 15 \times 4 \div (-10)$

   D. $(-4) \times (-9) + 4$

5) 432 inches equal to …?

    A. 36 ft.

    B. 110 ft.

    C. 55 ft.

    D. 25 ft.

6) Which of the following equations is true?

    A. $0.08 = \frac{8}{10}$

    B. $\frac{36}{100} = 0.036$

    C. $7.9 = \frac{79}{10}$

    D. $\frac{54}{6} = 0.9$

7) What is the greatest common factor of 14 and 42?

    A. 14

    B. 7

    C. 42

    D. 420

8) Which list shows the integer numbers listed in order from least to greatest?

    A. $-22, -15, -10, \ 10, 21, 28$

    B. $-10, -15, -22, 10, 28, 21$

    C. $-22, -10, -15, 10, 28, 21$

    D. $-15, -22, -10, 10, 21, 28$

9) Based on the table below, which of the following expressions represents any value of f in term of its corresponding value of x?

A. $f(x) = x + 1\frac{1}{2}$

B. $f(x) = 3x - 1\frac{1}{2}$

C. $f(x) = 3x + 2$

D. $f(x) = x - 2\frac{1}{2}$

x	1	1.5	2
$f(x)$	1.5	3	4.5

10) A football team won exactly 80% of the games it played during last session. Which of the following could be the total number of games the team played last season?

A. 34

B. 15

C. 42

D. 22

11) There are 66 blue marbles and 234 red marbles. We want to place these marbles in some boxes so that there is the same number of red marbles in each box and the same number of blue marbles in each of the boxes. How many boxes do we need?

A. 4

B. 18

C. 16

D. 6

12) Car A travels 128.3 km at a given time, while car B travels 2.5 times the distance car A travels at the same time. What is the distance car B travels during that time?

A. 230.50 km

B. 320.50 km

C. 230.25 km

D. 320.75 km

13) Which of the following expressions has the greatest value?

A. $4^4 - 3^5$

B. $5^3 - 4^3$

C. $6^3 - 5^3$

D. $4^4 - 5^3$

14) The diameter of a circle is 9π. What is the area of the circle?

A. $81\pi^2$

B. $\dfrac{81\pi^2}{2}$

C. $\dfrac{81\pi^3}{4}$

D. $\dfrac{9\pi^3}{4}$

15) Elise has x apples. Alvin has 45 apples, which is 15 apples less than number of apples Elise owns. If Baron has $\dfrac{1}{5}$ times as many apples as Elise has. How many apples does Baron have?

A. 32

B. 50

C. 24

D. 12

16) Find the perimeter of shape in the following figure? (all angles are right angles)

A. 68

B. 62

C. 64

D. 66

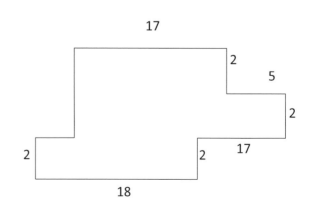

Session 2

❖ **Calculators are NOT permitted for this practice test.**

❖ **Time for Session 2: 60 Minutes**

17) In the following triangle find α.

A. 45°

B. 60°

C. 55°

D. 120°

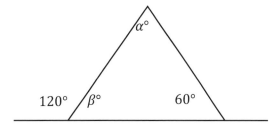

18) What is the probability of choosing a month starts with J in a year?

A. 1

B. $\frac{5}{8}$

C. $\frac{1}{6}$

D. $\frac{1}{4}$

19) $5(3.25) - 12.75 = \cdots$?

A. 3.75

B. 3.5

C. 2.75

D. 4.25

20) The perimeter of the trapezoid below is 49. What is its area?

A. 40 cm^2

B. 140 cm^2

C. 70 cm^2

D. 110 cm^2

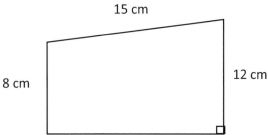

21) What are the values of mode and median in the following set of numbers?

$$1, 9, 1, 9, 8, 6, 7, 7, 11, 1, 8$$

A. Mode: 11, Median: 7

B. Mode: 6, Median: 1

C. Mode: 1, Median: 6

D. Mode: 1, Median: 7

22) The ratio of pens to pencils in a box is 2 to 3. If there are 110 pens and pencils in the box altogether, how many more pens should be put in the box to make the ratio of pens to pencils 1: 1?

A. 44

B. 22

C. 11

D. 66

23) Which of the following shows the numbers in increasing order?

A. $\frac{6}{5}, \frac{12}{4}, \frac{9}{12}, \frac{35}{6}$

B. $\frac{9}{12}, \frac{12}{4}, \frac{6}{5}, \frac{35}{6}$

C. $\frac{9}{12}, \frac{6}{5}, \frac{12}{4}, \frac{35}{6}$

D. $\frac{35}{6}, \frac{12}{4}, \frac{9}{12}, \frac{6}{5}$

24) If $6x - 2 = 40$, what is the value of $2x + 6$?

    A. 15

    B. 20

    C. 14

    D. 7

Types of air pollutions in 10 cities of a country

Type of Pollution	Number of Cities									
A	▓	▓	▓	▓	▓	▓	▓	▓		
B	▓	▓	▓	▓						
C	▓	▓	▓	▓	▓	▓	▓			
D	▓	▓	▓							
E	▓	▓	▓	▓	▓	▓	▓			
	1	2	3	4	5	6	7	8	9	10

25) Based on the above data, what percent of cities are in the type of pollution C,

  B, and E respectively?

  A. 60%, 40%, 70%

   B. 40%, 60%, 70%

   C. 70%, 40%, 60%

   D. 40%, 60%, 30%

26) How many tiles of 9 cm² is needed to cover a floor of dimension 4 cm by 45 cm?

   A. 45

   B. 36

   C. 24

   D. 20

27) A shaft rotates 540 times in 9 seconds. How many times does it rotate in 11 seconds?

   A. 640

   B. 660

   C. 460

   D. 600

28) Which of the following statement can describe the following inequality correctly?

$$\frac{x}{4} \geq 11$$

   A. David put x books in 4 shelves, and each shelf had at least 11 books.

   B. David placed 4 books in x shelves so that each shelf had less than 11 books.

   C. David put 11 books in x shelves and each shelf had exactly 4 books.

   D. David put x books in 4 shelves, and each shelf had more than 11 books

29) Removing which of the following numbers will change the average of the numbers to 8.4?   3, 6, 11, 12, 9, 7

A. 6

B. 7

C. 3

D. 11

30) If point A placed at $-\frac{12}{2}$ on a number line, which of the following points has a distance equal to 4 from point A?

A. -10

B. -2

C. 5

D. A and B

"This is the end of Practice Test 3"

The Florida Standards Assessments

FSA Practice Test 4

Mathematics

GRADE 6

Administered *Month Year*

Session 1

❖ **Calculators are NOT permitted for this practice test.**

❖ **Time for Session 2: 60 Minutes**

1) Martin earns $30 an hour. Which of the following inequalities represents the amount of time Martin needs to work per day to earn at least $430 per day?

   A. $30t \geq 430$

   B. $30t \leq 430$

   C. $30 + t \geq 430$

   D. $30 + t \leq 430$

2) What is the value of the expression $2(-4x - 2y) + (2 + 4x)^2$,, when $x = 1$ and $y = -3$?

   A. 28

   B. -40

   C. 40

   D. -28

3) Round $\frac{463}{8}$ to the nearest tenth.

   A. 56.8

   B. 58.8

   C. 57.9

   D. 59

4) Find the opposite of the numbers 12, 0.

A. $\frac{1}{12}, 0$

B. $-12, 3$

C. $-12, 0$

D. $-\frac{1}{12}, -3$

5) Which ordered pair describes point A that is shown below?

A. $(4, -2)$

B. $(-4, -2)$

C. $(-2, -4)$

D. $(-4, 2)$

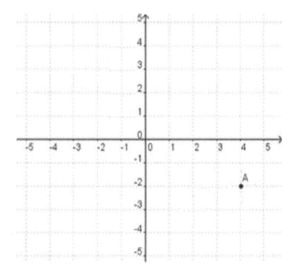

6) To produce a special concrete, for every 16 kg of cement, 4 liters of water is required. Which of the following ratios is the same as the ratio of cement to liters of water?

A. 80:20

B. 80:10

C. 24:12

D. 64:14

7) $(66 + 24) \div 15$ is equivalent to …

    A. $90 \div 2.4$

    B. $\frac{90}{15} + 15$

    C. $(2 \times 3 \times 3 \times 5) \div (3 \times 5)$

    D. $(2 \times 3 \times 3 \times 5) \div 3 + 5$

8) Which of the following graphs represents the following inequality?

$$-3 \le 4x - 3 < 5$$

    A.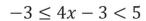

    B.

    C.

    D.

9) The ratio of boys to girls in a school is 3:5. If there are 400 students in the school, how many boys are in the school?

    A. 210

    B. 350

    C. 400

    D. 150

10) What is the volume of a box with the following dimensions? Height = 3cm

Width = 6 cm   Length = 5 cm

A. 120 cm^3

B. 18 cm^3

C. 30 cm^3

D. 90 cm^3

11) Anita's trick–or–treat bag contains 17 pieces of chocolate, 18 suckers, 15 pieces of gum, 12 pieces of licorice. If she randomly pulls a piece of candy from her bag, what is the probability of her pulling out a piece of sucker?

A. $\frac{1}{9}$

B. $\frac{9}{31}$

C. $\frac{3}{31}$

D. $\frac{18}{18} = 1$

12) Which statement is true about all rectangles?

A: Both diagonals have equal measure.

B: All sides are congruent.

C: Both diagonals are perpendicular.

D: All the statements are true

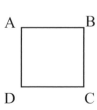

13) Which of the following lists shows the fractions in order from least to greatest?

$$\frac{3}{4}, \frac{1}{8}, \frac{14}{5}, \frac{28}{15}$$

A. $\frac{3}{4}, \frac{28}{15}, \frac{14}{5}, \frac{1}{8}$

B. $\frac{28}{15}, \frac{3}{4}, \frac{1}{8}, \frac{14}{5}$

C. $\frac{1}{8}, \frac{3}{4}, \frac{28}{15}, \frac{14}{5}$

D. $\frac{28}{15}, \frac{3}{4}, \frac{14}{5}, \frac{1}{8}$

14) Which statement about 3 multiplied by $\frac{5}{7}$ must be true?

A. The product is between 2 and 2.5

B. The product is greater than 1

C. The product is equal to $\frac{22}{15}$

D. The product is between 0.5 and 1

15) What is the equation of a line that passes through points (3, 1) and (5, 7)?

A. $y = 3x + 8$

B. $y = 3x - 8$

C. $y = 6x + 3$

D. $y = 6x - 3$

Session 2

❖ **Calculators are NOT permitted for this practice test.**

❖ **Time for Session 2: 60 Minutes**

16) The distance between two cities is 3,636 feet. What is the distance of the two cities in yards?

    A. 1,212 yd.

    B. 1,717 yd.

    C. 1,101 yd.

    D. 1,255 yd.

17) 109 is equal to …

    A. $-10 - (3 \times 15) + (7 \times 20)$

    B. $\left(\frac{13}{8} \times 40\right) + \left(\frac{96}{4}\right)$

    C. $\left(\left(\frac{15}{2} + \frac{27}{2}\right) \times 4\right) - \frac{24}{4} + \frac{124}{4}$

    D. $\frac{108}{9} + \frac{93}{3} + 20$

18) Mr. Jones saves $3,000 out of his monthly family income of $42,600. What fractional part of his income does Mr. Jones save?

    A. $\frac{1}{17}$

    B. $\frac{1}{71}$

    C. $\frac{5}{71}$

    D. $\frac{3}{17}$

19) If the area of the following trapezoid is equal to A, which equation represent x?

A. $x = \dfrac{14}{A}$

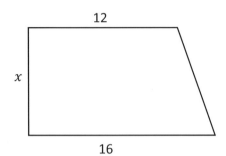

B. $x = \dfrac{A}{14}$

C. $x = A + 14$

D. $x = A - 14$

20) A car costing $700 is discounted 40%. Which of the following expressions can be used to find the selling price of the car?

A. $(700)(0.4)$

B. $700 - (700 \times 0.4)$

C. $(700)(0.6)$

D. $700 - (700 \times 0.6)$

21) When point A $(-4, 7)$ is reflected over the y-axis to get the point B, what are the coordinates of point B?

A. $(-4, -7)$

B. $(4, -7)$

C. $(4, 7)$

D. $(-4, 7)$

22) An integer is chosen at random from 1 to 20. Find the probability of not selecting a composite number?

A. $\frac{11}{20}$

B. $\frac{3}{5}$

C. $\frac{9}{20}$

D. $\frac{1}{5}$

23) By what factor did the number below change from first to fourth number?

$$11, \ 121, \ 1331, \ 14641$$

A. 11

B. 14

C. 121

D. 1,111

24) Based on the table below, which expression represents any value of f in term of its corresponding value of x?

A. $f(x) = 4x - \frac{7}{10}$

B. $f(x) = 3x + \frac{1}{8}$

C. $f(x) = 4x + 1\frac{1}{5}$

D. $f(x) = 5x + \frac{3}{10}$

x	0.5	1.5	3.25
$f(x)$	3.2	7.2	14.2

25) Calculate the approximate area of the following circle? (the diameter is 11)

A. 88

B. 190

C. 180

D. 360

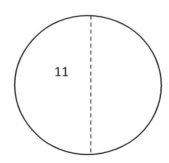

26) The following graph shows the mark of seven students in mathematics. What is the mean (average) of the marks?

A. 14.42

B. 14.93

C. 16.2

D. 15.05

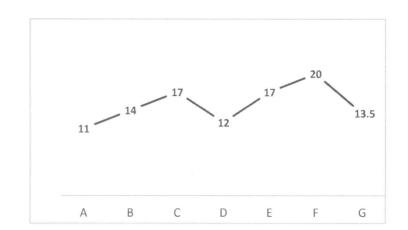

27) If the area of the following rectangular ABCD is 160, and E is the midpoint of AB, what is the area of the shaded part?

A. 90

B. 80

C. 40

D. 30

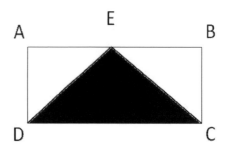

28) Which of the following statements is correct, according to the graph below?

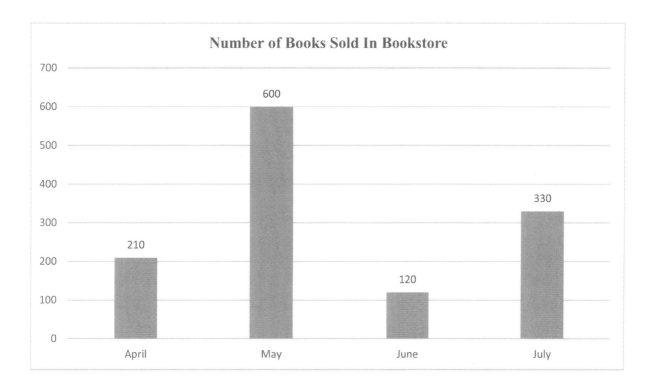

A. The number of books sold in the April was triple the number of books sold in the July.

B. The number of books sold in the July was less than one third the number of books sold in the May.

C. The number of books sold in the June was more than half the number of books sold in the April.

D. The number of books sold in the May was equal to the number of books sold in April plus the number of books sold in the June

29) What is the ratio between α and β, $\left(\frac{\alpha}{\beta}\right)$ in the following shape?

A. $\frac{2}{5}$

B. $\frac{5}{13}$

C. $\frac{3}{5}$

D. $\frac{5}{11}$

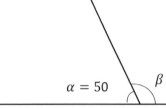

$\alpha = 50$ β

30) What is the lowest common multiple of 21 and 63?

A. 63

B. 45

C. 21

D. 7

"This is the end of Practice Test 4"

The Florida Standards Assessments

FSA Practice Test 5

Mathematics

GRADE 6

Administered *Month Year*

Session 1

❖ **Calculators are NOT permitted for this practice test.**

❖ **Time for Session 1: 60 Minutes**

1) If $x = -2$, which of the following equations is true?

   A. $x(5x - 4) = 30$

   B. $3(10 - x^2) = -16$

   C. $3(-3x + 5) = 30$

   D. $2x(-5x - 15) = 20$

2) What is the perimeter of the following shape? (it's a right triangle)

   A. 20 cm

   B. 10 cm

   C. 36 cm

   D. 24cm

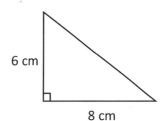

6 cm

8 cm

3) 70 is what percent of 40?

   A. 220 %

   B. 180 %

   C. 150 %

   D. 175 %

4) Which of the following expressions has a value of -18?

   A. $-6 + (-21 \div 7) + \frac{-8}{3} \times 3$

   B. $3 \times (-11) + (-4) \times 5$

   C. $(-3) + 12 \times 5 \div (-4)$

   D. $(-3) \times (-7) + 3$

5) 540 inches equal to …?

   A. 45 ft.

   B. 150 ft.

   C. 95 ft.

   D. 35 ft.

6) Which of the following equations is true?

   A. $0.09 = \frac{9}{10}$

   B. $\frac{45}{100} = 0.045$

   C. $5.3 = \frac{53}{10}$

   D. $\frac{42}{7} = 0.6$

7) What is the greatest common factor of 15 and 60?

   A. 15

   B. 12

   C. 60

   D. 900

8) Which list shows the integer numbers listed in order from least to greatest?

   A. $-16, -9, -4,\ 4, 18, 20$

   B. $-4, -9, -16, 4, 20, 18$

   C. $-16, -4, -9, 4, 20, 18$

   D. $-9, -16, -4, 4, 18, 20$

9) Based on the table below, which of the following expressions represents any value of f in term of its corresponding value of x?

x	3.1	4.2	5.9
$f(x)$	3.4	4.5	6.2

A. $f(x) = 2x - \frac{3}{10}$

B. $f(x) = x + \frac{3}{10}$

C. $f(x) = 2x + 2\frac{2}{5}$

D. $f(x) = 2x + \frac{3}{10}$

10) A football team won exactly 60% of the games it played during last session. Which of the following could be the total number of games the team played last season?

A. 64

B. 25

C. 46

D. 52

11) There are 84 blue marbles and 204 red marbles. We want to place these marbles in some boxes so that there is the same number of red marbles in each box and the same number of blue marbles in each of the boxes. How many boxes do we need?

A. 8

B. 11

C. 10

D. 12

12) Car A travels 243.26 km at a given time, while car B travels 3.5 times the distance car A travels at the same time. What is the distance car B travels during that time?

A. 651.41 km

B. 486.52 km

C. 641.22 km

D. 851.41 km

13) Which of the following expressions has the greatest value?

A. $5^4 - 7^3$

B. $8^3 - 3^5$

C. $6^4 - 4^5$

D. $9^3 - 13^2$

14) The diameter of a circle is 5 π. What is the area of the circle?

    A. $25\pi^2$

    B. $\dfrac{25\pi^2}{2}$

    C. $\dfrac{25\pi^3}{4}$

    D. $\dfrac{5\pi^3}{4}$

15) Elise has x apples. Alvin has 55 apples, which is 25 apples less than number of apples Elise owns. If Baron has $\dfrac{1}{4}$ times as many apples as Elise has. How many apples does Baron have?

    A. 22

    B. 55

    C. 25

    D. 20

16) Find the perimeter of shape in the following figure? (all angles are right angles)

    A. 48

    B. 56

    C. 28

    D. 58

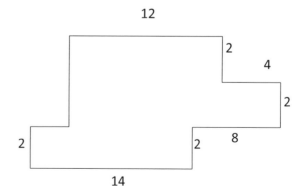

Session 2

❖ **Calculators are NOT permitted for this practice test.**

❖ **Time for Session 2: 60 Minutes**

17) In the following triangle find α.

A. 85°

B. 70°

C. 65°

D. 80°

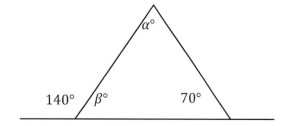

18) What is the probability of choosing a month starts with M in a year?

A. 1

B. $\frac{3}{4}$

C. $\frac{1}{3}$

D. $\frac{1}{6}$

19) $6(2.342) - 10.924 = \cdots$?

A. 3.491

B. 3.128

C. 4.128

D. 3.059

20) The perimeter of the trapezoid below is 53. What is its area?

A. 61 cm^2

B. 161 cm^2

C. 100 cm^2

D. 80 cm^2

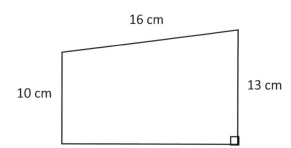

21) What are the values of mode and median in the following set of numbers?

$$2, 3, 3, 5, 5, 6, 7, 4, 2, 2, 4$$

A. Mode: 3, Median: 3.9

B. Mode: 1.2, Median: 2

C. Mode: 2, Median: 1

D. Mode: 2, Median: 4

22) The ratio of pens to pencils in a box is 4 to 6. If there are 180 pens and pencils in the box altogether, how many more pens should be put in the box to make the ratio of pens to pencils 1: 1?

A. 24

B. 36

C. 72

D. 108

23) Which of the following shows the numbers in increasing order?

A. $\dfrac{5}{2}, \dfrac{9}{3}, \dfrac{8}{15}, \dfrac{45}{8}$

B. $\dfrac{8}{15}, \dfrac{9}{3}, \dfrac{5}{2}, \dfrac{45}{8}$

C. $\dfrac{8}{15}, \dfrac{5}{2}, \dfrac{9}{3}, \dfrac{45}{8}$

D. $\dfrac{45}{8}, \dfrac{9}{3}, \dfrac{8}{15}, \dfrac{5}{2}$

24) If $5x - 4 = 16$, what is the value of $4x + 5$?

    A. 25

    B. 21

    C. 4

    D. 20

Types of air pollutions in 10 cities of a country

Type of Pollution	Number of Cities									
A										
B										
C										
D										
E										

    1 2 3 4 5 6 7 8 9 10

25) Based on the above data, what percent of cities are in the type of pollution C, B, and E respectively?

    A. 50%, 20%, 60%

    B. 20%, 50%, 30%

    C. 30%, 40%, 20%

    D. 20%, 50%, 30%

26) How many tiles of 7 cm^2 is needed to cover a floor of dimension 6 cm by 35 cm?

   A. 40

   B. 35

   C. 28

   D. 30

27) A shaft rotates 420 times in 7 seconds. How many times does it rotate in 13 seconds?

   A. 540

   B. 780

   C. 870

   D. 400

28) Which of the following statement can describe the following inequality correctly?

$$\frac{x}{7} \geq 9$$

   A. David put x books in 7 shelves, and each shelf had at least 9 books.

   B. David placed 7 books in x shelves so that each shelf had less than 9 books.

   C. David put 9 books in x shelves and each shelf had exactly 7 books.

   D. David put x books in 7 shelves, and each shelf had more than 9 books

29) Removing which of the following numbers will change the average of the numbers to 7.4?   2, 5, 10, 11, 8, 6

   A. 5

   B. 6

   C. 2

   D. 10

30) If point A placed at $-\frac{15}{3}$ on a number line, which of the following points has a distance equal to 8 from point A?

   A. −13

   B. 3

   C. −2

   D. A and B

"This is the end of Practice Test 5"

The Florida Standards Assessments

FSA Practice Test 6

Mathematics

GRADE 6

Administered *Month Year*

Session 1

❖ **Calculators are NOT permitted for this practice test.**

❖ **Time for Session 2: 60 Minutes**

1) Martin earns \$20 an hour. Which of the following inequalities represents the amount of time Martin needs to work per day to earn at least \$350 per day?

A. $20t \geq 350$

B. $20t \leq 350$

C. $20 + t \geq 350$

D. $20 + t \leq 350$

2) What is the value of the expression $3(2x - 3y) + (1 - 3x)^2$, when $x = 2$ and $y = -1$?

A. 31

B. -46

C. 46

D. -31

3) Round $\frac{565}{9}$ to the nearest tenth.

A. 62

B. 62.7

C. 62.8

D. 62.6

4) Find the opposite of the numbers 19, 0.

  A. $\frac{1}{19}, 0$

  B. $-19, 1$

  C. $-19, 0$

  D. $-\frac{1}{19}, 0$

5) Which ordered pair describes point A that is shown below?

  A. $(1, -3)$

  B. $(-1, -3)$

  C. $(-1, 3)$

  D. $(-1, -3)$

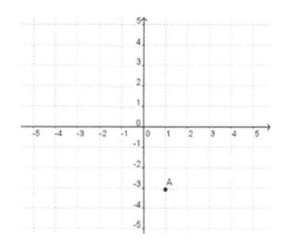

6) To produce a special concrete, for every 18 kg of cement, 3 liters of water is required. Which of the following ratios is the same as the ratio of cement to liters of water?

  A. 72:12

  B. 36:12

  C. 28:14

  D. 34:17

7) $(86 + 14) \div 20$ is equivalent to …

A. $100 \div 2.5$

B. $\frac{66}{6} + 6$

C. $(2 \times 2 \times 5 \times 5) \div (4 \times 5)$

D. $(2 \times 2 \times 5 \times 5) \div 4 + 5$

8) Which of the following graphs represents the following inequality?

$$-6 \le 2x - 8 < -4$$

A.

B.

C.

D.

9) The ratio of boys to girls in a school is 4:6. If there are 500 students in the school, how many boys are in the school?

A. 240

B. 300

C. 500

D. 200

10) What is the volume of a box with the following dimensions? Height = 4cm

Width = 7 cm   Length = 9 cm

A. 84 cm³

B. 126 cm³

C. 225 cm³

D. 252 cm³

11) Anita's trick–or–treat bag contains 18 pieces of chocolate, 20 suckers, 16 pieces of gum, 14 pieces of licorice. If she randomly pulls a piece of candy from her bag, what is the probability of her pulling out a piece of sucker?

A. $\frac{1}{20}$

B. $\frac{5}{17}$

C. $\frac{3}{20}$

D. $\frac{20}{20} = 1$

12) Which statement is true about all rectangles?

A: Both diagonals have equal measure.

B: All sides are congruent.

C: Both diagonals are perpendicular.

D: All the statements are true

13) Which of the following lists shows the fractions in order from least to greatest?

$$\frac{3}{5}, \frac{5}{7}, \frac{13}{6}, \frac{27}{30}$$

A. $\frac{27}{30}, \frac{5}{7}, \frac{3}{5}, \frac{13}{6}$

B. $\frac{5}{7}, \frac{27}{30}, \frac{13}{6}, \frac{3}{5}$

C. $\frac{3}{5}, \frac{5}{7}, \frac{27}{30}, \frac{13}{6}$

D. $\frac{27}{30}, \frac{5}{7}, \frac{13}{6}, \frac{3}{5}$

14) Which statement about 4 multiplied by $\frac{7}{9}$ must be true?

A. The product is between 2 and 2.5

B. The product is greater than 3

C. The product is equal to $\frac{81}{37}$

D. The product is between 1.5 and 2.5

15) What is the equation of a line that passes through points $(2, 3)$ and $(3, 8)$?

A. $y = 5x + 7$

B. $y = 5x - 7$

C. $y = 7x + 5$

D. $y = 7x - 5$

Session 2

❖ **Calculators are NOT permitted for this practice test.**

❖ **Time for Session 2: 60 Minutes**

16) The distance between two cities is 3,756 feet. What is the distance of the two cities in yards?

    A. 1,252 yd.

    B. 1,787 yd.

    C. 1,878 yd.

    D. 1,525 yd.

17) 150 is equal to …

    A. $-20 - (4 \times 11) + (8 \times 25)$

    B. $\left(\frac{13}{9} \times 99\right) + \left(\frac{156}{2}\right)$

    C. $\left(\left(\frac{19}{4} + \frac{35}{4}\right) \times 9\right) - \frac{25}{2} + \frac{164}{4}$

    D. $\frac{278}{6} + \frac{221}{3} + 50$

18) Mr. Jones saves \$3,800 out of his monthly family income of \$49,400. What fractional part of his income does Mr. Jones save?

    A. $\frac{1}{27}$

    B. $\frac{1}{14}$

    C. $\frac{1}{13}$

    D. $\frac{3}{13}$

19) If the area of the following trapezoid is equal to A, which equation represent x?

A. $x = \dfrac{13}{A}$

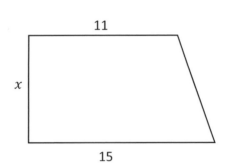

B. $x = \dfrac{A}{13}$

C. $x = A + 13$

D. $x = A - 13$

20) A car costing \$900 is discounted 30%. Which of the following expressions can be used to find the selling price of the car?

A. $(900)(0.4)$

B. $900 - (900 \times 0.3)$

C. $(900)(0.3)$

D. $900 - (900 \times 0.7)$

21) When point A $(-8, 9)$ is reflected over the y-axis to get the point B, what are the coordinates of point B?

A. $(-8, -9)$

B. $(8, -9)$

C. $(8, 9)$

D. $(-8, 9)$

22) An integer is chosen at random from 1 to 30. Find the probability of not selecting a composite number?

A. $\frac{11}{40}$

B. $\frac{3}{15}$

C. $\frac{11}{30}$

D. $\frac{1}{3}$

23) By what factor did the number below change from first to fourth number?

16, 256, 4096, 65536

A. 16

B. 15

C. 256

D. 4,096

24) Based on the table below, which expression represents any value of f in term of its corresponding value of x?

A. $f(x) = 2x - \frac{2}{5}$

B. $f(x) = x + \frac{2}{5}$

C. $f(x) = 3x + 3\frac{1}{5}$

D. $f(x) = 4x + \frac{4}{10}$

x	2.2	3.6	5.1
$f(x)$	9.8	14	18.5

25) Calculate the approximate area of the following circle? (the diameter is 13)

A. 98

B. 133

C. 156

D. 531

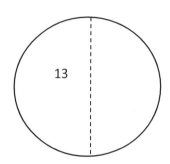

26) The following graph shows the mark of seven students in mathematics. What is the mean (average) of the marks?

A. 15.4

B. 14.07

C. 15.2

D. 16.05

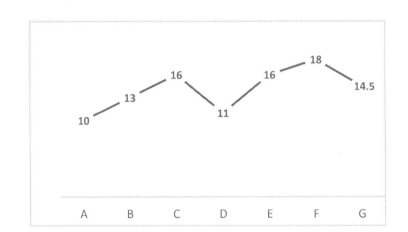

27) If the area of the following rectangular ABCD is 120, and E is the midpoint of AB, what is the area of the shaded part?

A. 50

B. 60

C. 80

D. 70

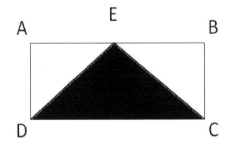

28) Which of the following statements is correct, according to the graph below?

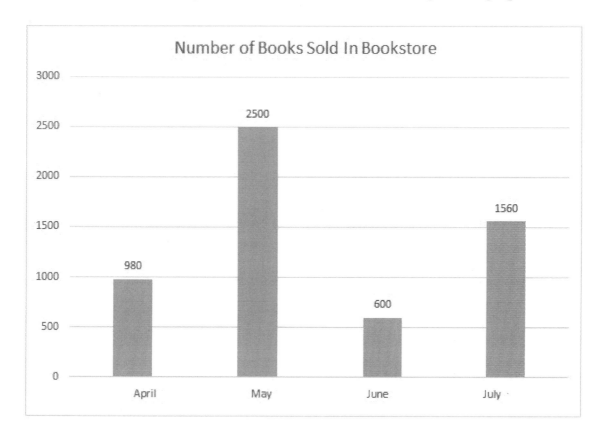

A. The number of books sold in the April was twice the number of books sold in the July.

B. The number of books sold in the July was less than half the number of books sold in the May.

C. The number of books sold in the June was more than half the number of books sold in the April.

D. The number of books sold in the July was equal to the number of books sold in April plus the number of books sold in the June

29) What is the ratio between α and β, $\left(\frac{\alpha}{\beta}\right)$ in the following shape?

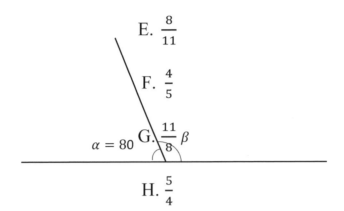

E. $\frac{8}{11}$

F. $\frac{4}{5}$

G. $\frac{11}{8}$

$\alpha = 80$ β

H. $\frac{5}{4}$

30) What is the lowest common multiple of 15 and 45?

A. 45

B. 90

C. 30

D. 35

"This is the end of Practice Test 6"

Answer Keys

FSA Practice Tests

❋ Now, it's time to review your results to see where you went wrong and what areas you need to improve!

Practice Test - 1						Practice Test - 2					
1	D	11	D	21	D	1	A	11	B	21	C
2	D	12	D	22	B	2	C	12	A	22	B
3	D	13	A	23	B	3	C	13	C	23	B
4	C	14	C	24	B	4	C	14	D	24	B
5	A	15	D	25	A	5	A	15	B	25	C
6	C	16	B	26	D	6	A	16	C	26	B
7	A	17	B	27	B	7	C	17	C	27	C
8	A	18	D	28	A	8	D	18	B	28	A
9	B	19	B	29	A	9	D	19	C	29	A
10	B	20	B	30	D	10	D	20	A	30	B

Practice Test - 3

1	D	11	D	21	D
2	D	12	D	22	B
3	D	13	D	23	C
4	C	14	C	24	B
5	A	15	D	25	A
6	C	16	B	26	D
7	A	17	B	27	B
8	A	18	D	28	A
9	B	19	B	29	A
10	B	20	B	30	D

Practice Test - 4

1	A	11	B	21	C
2	C	12	D	22	C
3	C	13	D	23	A
4	C	14	B	24	C
5	A	15	B	25	B
6	A	16	A	26	B
7	C	17	C	27	B
8	B	18	C	28	C
9	D	19	B	29	B
10	D	20	B	30	A

Practice Test - 5

1	D	11	D	21	D
2	D	12	D	22	B
3	D	13	D	23	C
4	C	14	C	24	B
5	A	15	D	25	A
6	C	16	B	26	D
7	A	17	B	27	B
8	A	18	D	28	A
9	B	19	B	29	A
10	B	20	B	30	D

Practice Test - 6

1	A	11	B	21	C
2	C	12	D	22	C
3	C	13	D	23	A
4	C	14	B	24	C
5	A	15	B	25	B
6	A	16	A	26	B
7	C	17	C	27	B
8	A	18	C	28	C
9	D	19	B	29	B
10	D	20	B	30	A

Answers and

Explanations

Practice Test 1

FSA - Mathematics

Answers and Explanations

1) Answer: D

Plugin the value of x in the equations. $x = -3$, then:

A. $x(4x - 1) = 35 \rightarrow -3(4(-3) - 1) = -3(-12 - 1) = -3(-13) = 39 \neq 35$

B. $2(12 - x^2) = -6 \rightarrow 2(12 - (-3)^2) = 2(12 - 9) = 2(3) \neq -6$

C. $4(-2x + 4) = 42 \rightarrow 4(-2(-3) + 4) = 4(6 + 4) = 40 \neq 42$

D. $x(-7x - 12) = -27 \rightarrow -3(-7(-3) - 12) = -3(21 - 12) = -27 = -27$

2) Answer: D

Use Pythagorean theorem to find the hypotenuse of the triangle.

$a^2 + b^2 = c^2 \rightarrow 3^2 + 4^2 = c^2 \rightarrow 9 + 16 = c^2 \rightarrow 25 = c^2 \rightarrow c = 5$

The perimeter of the triangle is: $3 + 4 + 5 = 12$

3) Answer: D

Use percent formula:

$\text{Part} = \frac{\text{percent}}{100} \times \text{whole}$

$60 = \frac{\text{percent}}{100} \times 25 \Rightarrow 60 = \frac{\text{percent} \times 25}{100} \Rightarrow$

$60 = \frac{\text{percent} \times 5}{20}$, multiply both sides by 20.

$1200 = \text{percent} \times 5$, divide both sides by 5.

$240 = \text{percent}$; The answer is 240%

4) Answer: C

Let's check the options provided.

A. $-5 + (-18 \div 3) + \frac{-6}{5} \times 5 \rightarrow -5 + (-6) + (-6) = -17$

B. $2 \times (-10) + (-3) \times 4 = (-20) + (-12) = -32$

C. $(-2) + 14 \times 3 \div (-7) = -2 + 42 \div (-7) = -2 - 6 = -8$

D. $(-4) \times (-8) + 5 = 32 + 5 = 37$

5) Answer: A

1 feet = 12 inches. Then: $420 \text{ in} \times \dfrac{1 \text{ ft}}{12 \text{ in}} = \dfrac{420}{12} \text{ ft} = 35 \text{ ft}$

6) Answer: C

A. $0.08 = \dfrac{8}{100}$

B. $\dfrac{30}{100} = \dfrac{2}{10} = 0.3$

C. $3.4 = 3\dfrac{4}{10} = \dfrac{34}{10}$

D. $\dfrac{35}{7} = 5$

7) Answer: A

Prime factorizing of $12 = 2 \times 2 \times 3$

Prime factorizing of $36 = 2 \times 3 \times 2 \times 3$

To find Greatest Common Factor, multiply the common factors of both numbers.

GCF$= 2 \times 2 \times 3 = 12$

8) Answer: A

$-15 < -6 < -3 < 3 < 8 < 10$; Then choice A

9) Answer: B

Plug in the values of x in the equations provided.

A. $f(x) = x + 1\dfrac{5}{2} = 1.2 + 1\dfrac{2}{5} = 1.2 + \dfrac{7}{2} = 4.7 \neq -2.3$

B. $f(x) = x - 1\dfrac{5}{2} = 1.2 - 1\dfrac{2}{5} = -2.3$

C. $f(x) = 2x + 1\dfrac{5}{2} = 2(1.2) + \dfrac{7}{2} = 5.9 \neq -2.3$

D. $f(x) = 2x - 1\dfrac{5}{2} = 2(1.2) - \dfrac{7}{2} = -1.1 \neq -2.3$

10) Answer: B

Choices A, C and D are incorrect because 60% of each of the numbers is a non-whole number.

A. 61, $70\% \text{ of } 61 = 0.70 \times 61 = 42.7$

B. 50, $70\% \text{ of } 50 = 0.70 \times 50 = 35$

C. 42, $70\% \text{ of } 42 = 0.70 \times 42 = 29.4$

D. 25, $70\% \ of \ 25 = 0.70 \times 25 = 17.5$

11) Answer: D

First, we need to find the GCF (Greatest Common Factor) of 154 and 44.

$154 = 11 \times 14$

$44 = 4 \times 11 \rightarrow GFC = 11$; Therefore, we need 11 boxes.

12) Answer: D

Distance that car B travels = 2.2 × distance that car A travels

$= 2.2 \times 341.26 = 750.8 \ Km$

13) Answer: A

A. $5^3 - 4^3 = 125 - 64 = 61$

B. $2^5 - 2^2 = 32 - 4 = 28$

C. $3^4 - 5^2 = 81 - 25 = 56$

D. $4^4 - 15^2 = 256 - 225 = 31$

14) Answer: C

The radius of the circle is: $\dfrac{3\pi}{2}$

The area of circle: $\pi r^2 = \pi (\dfrac{3\pi}{2})^2 = \pi \times \dfrac{9\pi^2}{4} = \dfrac{9\pi^3}{4}$

15) Answer: D

Elise has x apple which is 20 apples more than number of apples Alvin owns.

Therefore: $x - 20 = 45 \rightarrow x = 45 + 20 = 65$

Elise has 65 apples.

Let y be the number of apples that Baron has. Then: $y = \dfrac{1}{5} \times 65 = 13$

16) Answer: B

Let x and y be two sides of the shape. Then:

$x + 1 = 1 + 1 + 1 \rightarrow x = 2$

$y + 6 + 2 = 7 + 4 \rightarrow y + 8 = 11 \rightarrow y = 3$

Then, the perimeter is:

$1 + 7 + 1 + 4 + 1 + 2 + 1 + 6 + 2 + 3 = 28$

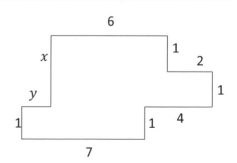

17)Answer: B

Complementary angles add up to 180 degrees.

$$\beta + 160° = 180° \rightarrow \beta = 180° - 160° = 20°$$

The sum of all angles in a triangle is 180 degrees. Then:

$$\alpha + \beta + 65° = 180° \rightarrow \alpha + 20° + 65° = 180°$$

$$\rightarrow \alpha + 85° = 180° \rightarrow \alpha = 180° - 85° = 95°$$

18)Answer: D

Two months, April and August, in 12 months start with A, then:

$$\text{Probability} = \frac{number\ of\ desired\ outcomes}{number\ of\ total\ outcomes} = \frac{2}{12} = \frac{1}{6}$$

19)Answer: B

$$5(1.153) - 2.126 = 5.765 - 2.126 = 3.639$$

20)Answer: B

The perimeter of the trapezoid is 48.

Therefore, the missing side (height) is $= 48 - 8 - 12 - 16 = 12$

Area of the trapezoid: $A = \frac{1}{2}h(b1 + b2) = \frac{1}{2}(12)(8 + 12) = 120$

21)Answer: D

First, put the numbers in order from least to greatest: 1, 1, 1, 2, 2, 3, 3, 4, 4, 5, 6

The Mode of the set of numbers is: 1 (the most frequent numbers)

Median is: 3 (the number in the middle)

22)Answer: B

The ratio of pens to pencils is 5: 7. Therefore there are 5 pens out of all 12 pens and pencils. To find the answer, first dived 144 by 12 then multiply the result by 5.

$$144 \div 12 = 12 \rightarrow 12 \times 5 = 60$$

There are 60 pens and 84 pencils (144-60). Therefore, 24 more pens should be put in the box to make the ratio 1: 1

23)Answer: B

$$\frac{35}{8} \cong 4.38 \qquad \frac{7}{4} = 1.75 \qquad \frac{9}{12} = 0.75 \qquad \frac{4}{2} = 2$$

Then: $\frac{9}{12} < \frac{7}{4} < \frac{4}{2} < \frac{35}{8}$

24) Answer: B

$3x - 2 = 16 \rightarrow 3x = 16 + 2 = 18 \rightarrow x = \frac{18}{3} = 9$

Then, $3x + 2 = 3(9) + 2 = 27 + 2 = 29$

25) Answer: A

Percent of cities in the type of pollution C: $\frac{4}{10} \times 100 = 40\%$

Percent of cities in the type of pollution B: $\frac{3}{10} \times 100 = 30\%$

Percent of cities in the type of pollution E: $\frac{7}{10} \times 100 = 70\%$

26) Answer: D

The area of the floor is: 8 cm × 25 cm = 200 cm

The number of tiles needed = 200 ÷ 5 = 40

27) Answer: B

The shaft rotates 360 times in 9 seconds. Then, the number of rotates in 16 second equals to: $\frac{360 \times 16}{9} = 640$

28) Answer: A

Let's write an inequality for each statement.

A. $\frac{x}{6} \geq 8$ (this is the same as the inequality provided)

B. $\frac{6}{x} < 8$

C. $\frac{8}{x} = 6$

D. $\frac{x}{6} > 8$

29) Answer: A

Check each option provided:

A. 6 $\frac{1+4+7+13+15}{5} = \frac{40}{5} = 8$

B. 15 $\frac{1+4+7+13+6}{5} = \frac{31}{5} = 6.2$

C. 7 $\frac{1+4+13+15+6}{5} = \frac{39}{5} = 7.8$

D. 12 $\quad \frac{1+4+7+6+15}{5} = \frac{33}{5} = 6.6$

30) Answer: D

If the value of point A is greater than the value of point B, then the distance of two points on the number line is: value of A− value of B

A. $-\frac{16}{4} - (-10) = -4 + 10 = 6 = 6$

B. $2 - \left(-\frac{16}{4}\right) = 2 + 4 = 6 = 6$

C. $-3 - \left(-\frac{16}{4}\right) = -3 + 4 = 1 \neq 6$

Practice Test 2

FSA - Mathematics

Answers and Explanations

1) Answer: A

For one hour he earns \$30, then for t hours he earns \$30t. If he wants to earn at least \$250, therefor, the number of working hours multiplied by 30must be equal to 250 or more than 250.

$$30t \geq 250$$

2) Answer: C

Plug in the value of x and y and use order of operations rule.

$x = 1$ and $y = -2$

$4(3x - 2y) + (4 - 5x)^2 = 4(3(1) - 2(-2)) + (4 - 5(1))^2 = 4(3 + 4) + (-1)^2 =$

$28 + 1 = 29$

3) Answer: C

$$\frac{415}{9} \cong 46.11 \cong 46.1$$

4) Answer: C

Opposite number of any number x is a number that if added to x, the result is 0. Then:

$16 + (-16) = 0$ and $0 + 0 = 0$

5) Answer: A

The coordinate plane has two axes. The vertical line is called the y-axis and the horizontal is called the x-axis. The points on the coordinate plane are address using the form (x, y). The point A is one unit on the left side of x-axis; therefore, its x value is 3 and it is two units up, therefore its y axis is -2. The coordinate of the point is: $(3, -2)$

6) Answer: A

$84: 12 = 14: 2$

$14 \times 6 = 84$ And $2 \times 6 = 12$

7) Answer: C

$(75 + 5) \div (16) = (80) \div (16)$

The prime factorization of 80 is: $2 \times 2 \times 2 \times 5$

The prime factorization of 16 is: 4×4

Therefore: $(80) \div (16) = (2 \times 2 \times 2 \times 5) \div (4 \times 4)$

8) Answer: D

Solve for x.

$-2 \le 2x - 4 < 8 \Rightarrow$ (add 4 all sides) $-2 + 4 \le 2x - 4 + 4 < 8 + 4 \Rightarrow$

$2 \le 2x < 12 \Rightarrow$ (divide all sides by 2) $1 \le x < 6$

x is between 1 and 6. Choice D represent this inequality.

9) Answer: D

The ratio of boy to girls is 5:7. Therefore, there are 5 boys out of 12 students. To find the answer, first divide the total number of students by 12, then multiply the result by 5.

$900 \div 12 = 75 \Rightarrow 75 \times 5 = 375$

10) Answer: D

Volume of a box = length × width × height = $8 \times 6 \times 5 = 240$

11) Answer: B

$\text{Probability} = \dfrac{number\ of\ desired\ outcomes}{number\ of\ total\ outcomes} = \dfrac{18}{16+18+14+12} = \dfrac{18}{60} = \dfrac{3}{10}$

12) Answer: A

In any rectangle, both diagonals have equal measure.

13) Answer: C

Let's compare each fraction: $\dfrac{3}{4} < \dfrac{4}{5} < \dfrac{26}{29} < \dfrac{11}{5}$

Only choice C provides the right order.

14) Answer: D

$3 \times \dfrac{5}{7} = \dfrac{15}{7} = 2.14$

A. $2.14 > 2$

B. $2.14 < 3$

C. $\frac{77}{25} = 3.08 \neq 2.4$

D. $2 < 2.14 < 2.3$ This is the answer!

15) Answer: B

The slope of the line is: $\frac{y_2 - y_1}{x_2 - x_1} = \frac{9-5}{4-0} = \frac{4}{4} = 1$

The equation of a line can be written as:

$$y - y_0 = m(x - x_0) \to y - 5 = 1(x - 0) \to y - 5 = 1x \to y = x + 5$$

16) Answer: C

Simplify each option provided.

A. $-10 - (5 \times 10) + (7 \times 20) = -10 - 50 + 140 = 80$

B. $\left(\frac{12}{8} \times 96\right) + \left(\frac{156}{6}\right) = 144 + 26 = 170$

C. $\left(\left(\frac{18}{4} + \frac{30}{4}\right) \times 8\right) - \frac{13}{2} + \frac{88}{4} = \left(\left(\frac{18+30}{4}\right) \times 8\right) - \frac{6}{2} + \frac{44}{2} = \left(\left(\frac{48}{4}\right) \times 8\right) + \frac{44-6}{2} =$

$(12 \times 8) + \frac{38}{2} = 96 + 19 = 115$ (this is the answer)

D. $\frac{481}{6} + \frac{121}{3} + 50 = \frac{481+242}{6} + 50 = 120.5 + 50 = 170.5$

17) Answer: C

2,700 out of 74,700 equals to $\frac{2,700}{74,700} = \frac{3}{83}$

18) Answer: B

The area of the trapezoid is: $area = \frac{(base\ 1 + base\ 2)}{2} \times height = \left(\frac{14+16}{2}\right) x = A \to$

$15x = A \to x = \frac{A}{15}$

19) Answer: C

There are 40 integers from 1 to 40. Set of numbers that are not composite between 1 and 40 is: A= {1, 2, 3, 5, 7, 11, 13, 17, 19, 23, 29,31,37}

13 integers are not composite. Probability of not selecting a composite number is:

Probability $= \frac{number\ of\ desired\ outcomes}{number\ of\ total\ outcomes} = \frac{13}{40}$

20) Answer: A

$\frac{168}{12} = 14, \frac{2352}{168} = 14, \frac{32928}{2352} = 14$; Therefore, the factor is 14

21) Answer: C

Plug in the value of x into the function $f(x)$. First, plug in 3.1 for x.

A. $f(x) = 2x - \frac{3}{10} = 2(3.1) - \frac{3}{10} = 5.9 \neq 8.6$

B. $f(x) = x + \frac{3}{10} = 3.1 + \frac{3}{10} = 3.4 \neq 10.8$

C. $f(x) = 2x + 2\frac{2}{5} = 2(3.1) + 2\frac{2}{5} = 6.2 + 2.4 = 8.6$ This is correct!

Plug in other values of x. $x = 4.2$

$f(x) = 2x + 2\frac{2}{5} = 2(4.2) + 2.4 = 10.8$ This one is also correct. $x = 5.9$

$f(x) = 2x + 2\frac{2}{5} = 2(5.9) + 2.4 = 14.2$ This one works too!

D. $2x + \frac{3}{10} = 2(3.1) + \frac{3}{10} = 6.5 \neq 8.6$

22) Answer: B

The diameter of a circle is twice the radius. Radius of the circle is $\frac{15}{2}$.

Area of a circle $= \pi r^2 = \pi(\frac{15}{2})^2 = 56.25\pi = 56.25 \times 3.14 = 176.625 \cong 177$

23) Answer: B

Average (mean) $= \frac{\text{sum of terms}}{\text{number of terms}} = \frac{12+13+16+13+15+20+13.5}{7} = 14.64$

24) Answer: B

Since, E is the midpoint of AB, then the area of all triangles DAE, DEF, CFE and CBE are equal.

Let x be the area of one of the triangles, then: $4x = 160 \rightarrow x = 40$

The area of DEC $= 2x = 2(40) = 80$

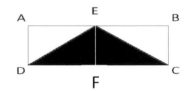

25) Answer: C

A. Number of books sold in April is: 490

    Number of books sold in July is: $780 \rightarrow \frac{490}{780} = \frac{49}{78} \neq 2$

B. Number of books sold in July is: 780

    Half the number of books sold in May is: $\frac{1250}{2} = 625 \rightarrow 780 > 625$

C. Number of books sold in June is: 300

   Half the number of books sold in April is: $\frac{490}{2} = 245 \rightarrow 300 > 245$ (it's correct)

D. $490 + 300 = 790 > 780$

26) Answer: B

α and β are complementary angles. The sum of complementary angles is 180 degrees.

$\alpha + \beta = 180° \rightarrow \beta = 180° - \alpha = 180° - 70° = 110°$

Then, $\frac{\alpha}{\beta} = \frac{70}{110} = \frac{7}{11}$

27) Answer: C

When points are reflected over y-axis, the value of y in the coordinates doesn't change and the sign of x changes. Therefore, the coordinates of point B is $(6, 4)$.

28) Answer: A

1 yard = 3 feet

Therefore, $4{,}389 \text{ ft.} \times \frac{1 \text{ yd}}{3 \text{ ft}} = 1{,}463 \text{ yd}$

29) Answer: A

Prime factorizing of $30 = 2 \times 3 \times 5$

Prime factorizing of $18 = 3 \times 2 \times 3$

LCM $= 2 \times 3 \times 3 \times 5 = 90$

30) Answer: B

To find the discount, multiply the number $(100\% - \text{rate of discount})$

Therefore; $600(100\% - 20\%) = 600(1 - 0.2) = 600 - (600 \times 0.2)$

Practice Test 3

FSA - Mathematics

Answers and Explanations

1) Answer: D

Plugin the value of x in the equations. $x = -5$, then:

A. $x(3x + 9) = 45 \rightarrow -5(3(-5) + 9) = -5(-15 + 9) = -5(-6) = 30 \neq 45$

B. $3(32 - x^2) = -18 \rightarrow 3(32 - (-5)^2) = 3(32 - 25) = 3(7) = 21 \neq -18$

C. $2(-5x - 10) = 55 \rightarrow 2(-5(-5) - 10) = 2(25 - 10) = 2(15) = 30 \neq 55$

D. $x(2x + 5) = 25 \rightarrow -5(2(-5) + 5) = -5(-10 + 5) = -5(-5) = 25 = 25$

2) Answer: D

Use Pythagorean theorem to find the hypotenuse of the triangle.

$$a^2 + b^2 = c^2 \rightarrow 5^2 + 12^2 = c^2 \rightarrow 25 + 144 = c^2 \rightarrow 169 = c^2 \rightarrow c = 13$$

The perimeter of the triangle is: $5 + 12 + 13 = 30$

3) Answer: D

Use percent formula:

$$Part = \frac{percent}{100} \times whole$$

$$63 = \frac{percent}{100} \times 30 \Rightarrow 63 = \frac{percent \times 30}{100} \Rightarrow$$

$63 = \frac{percent \times 3}{10}$, multiply both sides by 3.

$630 = percent \times 3$, divide both sides by 3.

$210 = percent$; The answer is 210%

4) Answer: C

Let's check the options provided.

A. $-8 + (-32 \div 8) + \frac{-5}{6} \times 6 \rightarrow -8 + (-4) + (-5) = -17$

B. $4 \times (-10) + (-6) \times 3 = (-40) + (-18) = -58$

C. $(-5) + 15 \times 4 \div (-10) = -5 + 60 \div (-10) = -5 - 6 = -11$

D. $(-4) \times (-9) + 4 = 36 + 4 = 40$

5) Answer: A

1 feet = 12 inches. Then: $432 \text{ in} \times \frac{1 \text{ ft}}{12 \text{ in}} = \frac{432}{12} \text{ ft} = 36 \text{ ft}$

6) Answer: C

A. $0.08 = \frac{8}{100}$

B. $\frac{36}{100} = \frac{9}{25} = 0.36$

C. $7.9 = 7\frac{9}{10} = \frac{79}{10}$

D. $\frac{54}{6} = 9$

7) Answer: A

Prime factorizing of $14 = 2 \times 7$

Prime factorizing of $42 = 2 \times 3 \times 7$

To find Greatest Common Factor, multiply the common factors of both numbers.

GCF$= 2 \times 7 = 14$

8) Answer: A

$-22 < -15 < -10 < 10 < 21 < 28$; Then choice A

9) Answer: B

Plug in the values of x in the equations provided.

A. $f(x) = x + 1\frac{1}{2} = 1 + 1\frac{1}{2} = 1 + \frac{3}{2} = 4.5 \neq 1.5$

B. $f(x) = 3x - 1\frac{1}{2} = 3(1) - \frac{3}{2} = 1.5$

C. $f(x) = 3x + 2 = 3(1) + 2 = 5 \neq 1.5$

D. $f(x) = x - 2\frac{1}{2} = 1 - \frac{5}{2} = -1.5 \neq 1.5$

10) Answer: B

Choices A, C and D are incorrect because 80% of each of the numbers is a non-whole number.

A. 34, $80\% \text{ of } 34 = 0.80 \times 34 = 27.2$

B. 15, $80\% \text{ of } 15 = 0.80 \times 15 = 12$

C. 42, $80\% \text{ of } 42 = 0.80 \times 42 = 33.6$

D. 22, $80\% \ of \ 22 = 0.80 \times 22 = 17.6$

11) Answer: D

First, we need to find the GCF (Greatest Common Factor) of 234 and 66.

$234 = 2 \times 3 \times 3 \times 13$

$66 = 2 \times 3 \times 11 \rightarrow$ GCF $= 2 \times 3 = 6$; Therefore, we need 6 boxes.

12) Answer: D

Distance that car B travels $= 2.5 \times$ distance that car A travels

$= 2.5 \times 128.3 = 320.75$ Km

13) Answer: D

A. $4^4 - 3^5 = 256 - 243 = 13$

B. $5^3 - 4^3 = 125 - 64 = 61$

C. $6^3 - 5^3 = 216 - 125 = 91$

D. $4^4 - 5^3 = 256 - 125 = 131$

14) Answer: C

The radius of the circle is: $\dfrac{9\pi}{2}$

The area of circle: $\pi r^2 = \pi(\dfrac{9\pi}{2})^2 = \pi \times \dfrac{81\pi^2}{4} = \dfrac{81\pi^3}{4}$

15) Answer: D

Elise has x apple which is 15 apples more than number of apples Alvin owns.

Therefore: $x - 15 = 45 \rightarrow x = 45 + 15 = 60$

Elise has 60 apples.

Let y be the number of apples that Baron has. Then: $y = \dfrac{1}{5} \times 60 = 12$

16) Answer: B

Let x and y be two sides of the shape. Then:

$x + 2 = 2 + 2 + 2 \rightarrow x = 4$

$y + 17 + 5 = 18 + 7 \rightarrow y + 22 = 25 \rightarrow y = 3$

Then, the perimeter is:

$2 + 18 + 2 + 7 + 2 + 5 + 2 + 17 + 4 + 3 = 62$

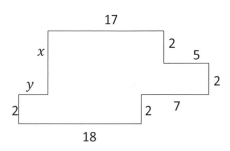

17) Answer: B

Complementary angles add up to 180 degrees.

$\beta + 120° = 180° \rightarrow \beta = 180° - 120° = 60°$

The sum of all angles in a triangle is 180 degrees. Then:

$\alpha + \beta + 70° = 180° \rightarrow \alpha + 60° + 60° = 180°$

$\rightarrow \alpha + 120° = 180° \rightarrow \alpha = 180° - 120° = 60°$

18) Answer: D

Three months, June and July and January, in 12 months start with J, then:

$\text{Probability} = \dfrac{number\ of\ desired\ outcomes}{number\ of\ total\ outcomes} = \dfrac{3}{12} = \dfrac{1}{4}$

19) Answer: B

$5(3.25) - 12.75 = 16.25 - 12.75 = 3.5$

20) Answer: B

The perimeter of the trapezoid is 49.

Therefore, the missing side (height) is $= 49 - 15 - 8 - 12 = 14$

Area of the trapezoid: $A = \dfrac{1}{2}h(b1 + b2) = \dfrac{1}{2}(14)(8 + 12) = 140$

21) Answer: D

First, put the numbers in order from least to greatest: 1, 1, 1, 6, 7, 7, 8, 8, 9, 9, 11

The Mode of the set of numbers is: 1 (the most frequent numbers)

Median is: 7 (the number in the middle)

22) Answer: B

The ratio of pens to pencils is 2: 3. Therefore there are 2 pens out of all 5 pens and pencils. To find the answer, first dived 180 by 5 then multiply the result by 2.

$110 \div 5 = 22 \rightarrow 22 \times 2 = 44$

There are 44 pens and 66 pencils (110–44) Therefore, 22 more pens should be put in the box to make the ratio 1: 1

23) Answer: C

$\dfrac{35}{6} \cong 5.83 \qquad \dfrac{6}{5} = 1.2 \qquad \dfrac{9}{12} \cong 0.75 \qquad \dfrac{12}{4} = 3$

Then: $\frac{9}{12} < \frac{6}{5} < \frac{12}{4} < \frac{35}{6}$

24) Answer: B

$$6x - 2 = 40 \rightarrow 6x = 40 + 2 = 42 \rightarrow x = \frac{42}{6} = 7$$

Then, $2x + 6 = 2(7) + 6 = 14 + 6 = 20$

25) Answer: A

Percent of cities in the type of pollution C: $\frac{6}{10} \times 100 = 60\%$

Percent of cities in the type of pollution B: $\frac{4}{10} \times 100 = 40\%$

Percent of cities in the type of pollution E: $\frac{7}{10} \times 100 = 70\%$

26) Answer: D

The area of the floor is: $4 \text{ cm} \times 45 \text{ cm} = 180 \text{ cm}^2$

The number of tiles needed $= 180 \div 9 = 20$

27) Answer: B

The shaft rotates 540 times in 9 seconds. Then, the number of rotates in 11 second equals to: $\frac{540 \times 11}{9} = 660$

28) Answer: A

Let's write an inequality for each statement.

A. $\frac{x}{4} \geq 11$ (this is the same as the inequality provided)

B. $\frac{4}{x} < 11$

C. $\frac{11}{x} = 4$

D. $\frac{x}{4} > 11$

29) Answer: A

Check each option provided:

A. 6 $\frac{3+7+9+11+12}{5} = \frac{42}{5} = 8.4$

B. 7 $\frac{3+6+9+11+12}{5} = \frac{41}{5} = 8.2$

C. 3 $\qquad \frac{6+7+9+11+12}{5} = \frac{45}{5} = 9$

D. 11 $\qquad \frac{3+6+7+9+12}{5} = \frac{37}{5} = 7.4$

30) Answer: D

If the value of point A is greater than the value of point B, then the distance of two points on the number line is: value of A− value of B

A. $-\frac{12}{2} - (-10) = -6 + 10 = 4 = 4$

B. $-2 - \left(-\frac{12}{2}\right) = -2 + 6 = 4 = 4$

C. $5 - \left(-\frac{12}{2}\right) = 5 + 6 = 11 \neq 4$

Practice Test 4

FSA - Mathematics

Answers and Explanations

1) Answer: A

For one hour he earns \$30, then for t hours he earns \$30t. If he wants to earn at least \$430, therefor, the number of working hours multiplied by 30 must be equal to 430 or more than 430.

$$30t \geq 430$$

2) Answer: C

Plug in the value of x and y and use order of operations rule.

$x = 1$ and $y = -3$

$2(-4x - 2y) + (2 + 4x)^2 = 2(-4(1) - 2(-3)) + (2 + 4(1))^2 = 2(-4 + 6) + (6)^2 = 4 + 36 = 40$

3) Answer: C

$$\frac{463}{8} \cong 57.875 \cong 57.9$$

4) Answer: C

Opposite number of any number x is a number that if added to x, the result is 0. Then:

$12 + (-12) = 0$ and $0 + 0 = 0$

5) Answer: A

The coordinate plane has two axes. The vertical line is called the y-axis and the horizontal is called the x-axis. The points on the coordinate plane are address using the form (x, y). The point A is four unit on the right side of x-axis; therefore, its x value is 4 and it is two units down, therefore its y axis is -2. The coordinate of the point is: $(4, -2)$

6) Answer: A

$80 : 20 = 16 : 4$

$16 \times 5 = 80$ \qquad And \qquad $4 \times 5 = 20$

7) Answer: C

$(66 + 24) \div (15) = (90) \div (15)$

The prime factorization of 90 is: $2 \times 3 \times 3 \times 5$

The prime factorization of 15 is: 3×5

Therefore: $(90) \div (15) = (2 \times 3 \times 3 \times 5) \div (3 \times 5)$

8) Answer: B

Solve for x.

$-3 \leq 4x - 3 < 5 \Rightarrow$ (add 3 all sides) $-3 + 3 \leq 2x - 3 + 3 < 5 + 3 \Rightarrow$

$0 \leq 4x < 8 \Rightarrow$ (divide all sides by 4) $0 \leq x < 2$

x is between 0 and 2. Choice B represent this inequality.

9) Answer: D

The ratio of boy to girls is 3:5. Therefore, there are 3 boys out of 8 students. To find the answer, first divide the total number of students by 8, then multiply the result by 3.

$400 \div 8 = 50 \Rightarrow 50 \times 3 = 150$

10) Answer: D

Volume of a box = length × width × height = $3 \times 6 \times 5 = 90$

11) Answer: B

$\text{Probability} = \dfrac{\textit{number of desired outcomes}}{\textit{number of total outcomes}} = \dfrac{18}{17+18+15+12} = \dfrac{18}{62} = \dfrac{9}{31}$

12) Answer: D

All the statements are true.

13) Answer: C

Let's compare each fraction: $\dfrac{1}{8} < \dfrac{3}{4} < \dfrac{28}{15} < \dfrac{14}{5}$

Only choice C provides the right order.

14) Answer: B

$3 \times \dfrac{5}{7} = \dfrac{15}{7} = 1.14$

A. $1.14 < 2$

B. $1.14 > 1$ This is the answer!

C. $\frac{22}{15} = 1.46 \neq 1.14$

D. $1 < 1.14$

15) Answer: B

The slope of the line is: $\frac{y_2 - y_1}{x_2 - x_1} = \frac{7-1}{5-3} = \frac{6}{2} = 3$

The equation of a line can be written as:

$y - y_0 = m(x - x_0) \rightarrow y - 1 = 3(x - 3) \rightarrow y - 1 = 3x - 9 \rightarrow y = 3x - 8$

16) Answer: A

1 yard = 3 feet

Therefore, $3{,}636 \text{ ft.} \times \frac{1\,\text{yd}}{3\,\text{ft}} = 1{,}212\text{yd}$

17) Answer: C

Simplify each option provided.

A. $-10 - (3 \times 15) + (7 \times 20) = -10 - 45 + 140 = 85$

B. $\left(\frac{13}{8} \times 40\right) + \left(\frac{96}{4}\right) = 65 + 24 = 89$

C. $\left(\left(\frac{15}{2} + \frac{27}{2}\right) \times 4\right) - \frac{24}{4} + \frac{124}{4} = \left(\left(\frac{15+27}{2}\right) \times 4\right) - \frac{24}{4} + \frac{124}{4} =$

$\left(\left(\frac{42}{2}\right) \times 4\right) + \frac{124-24}{4} = (21 \times 4) + \frac{100}{4} = 84 + 25 = 109$ (this is the answer)

D. $\frac{108}{9} + \frac{93}{3} + 20 = \frac{108+279}{9} + 20 = 43 + 20 = 63$

18) Answer: C

$3{,}000$ out of $42{,}600$ equals to $\frac{3{,}000}{42{,}600} = \frac{5}{71}$

19) Answer: B

The area of the trapezoid is: $area = \frac{(base\ 1 + base\ 2)}{2} \times height = \left(\frac{12+16}{2}\right)x = A \rightarrow$

$14x = A \rightarrow x = \frac{A}{14}$

20) Answer: B

To find the discount, multiply the number $(100\% - \text{rate of discount})$

Therefore; $700(100\% - 40\%) = 700(1 - 0.4) = 700 - (700 \times 0.4)$

21) Answer: C

When points are reflected over y-axis, the value of y in the coordinates doesn't change and the sign of x changes. Therefore, the coordinates of point B is $(4, 7)$.

22) Answer: C

There are 30 integers from 1 to 20. Set of numbers that are not composite between 1 and 20 is: A= {1, 2, 3, 5, 7, 11, 13, 17, 19}

9 integers are not composite. Probability of not selecting a composite number is:

$$\text{Probability} = \frac{number\ of\ desired\ outcomes}{number\ of\ total\ outcomes} = \frac{9}{20}$$

23) Answer: A

$\frac{121}{11} = 11, \frac{1,331}{121} = 11, \frac{14,641}{1,331} = 11$; Therefore, the factor is 11

24) Answer: C

Plug in the value of x into the function $f(x)$. First, plug in 0.5 for x.

A. $f(x) = 4x - \frac{7}{10} = 4(0.5) - \frac{7}{10} = 1.3 \neq 3.2$

B. $f(x) = 3x + \frac{1}{8} = 3(0.5) + \frac{1}{8} = 1.625 \neq 3.2$

C. $f(x) = 4x + 1\frac{1}{5} = 4(0.5) + 1\frac{1}{5} = 2 + 1.2 = 3.2$ This is correct!

Plug in other values of x. $x = 1.5$

$f(x) = 4x + 1\frac{1}{5} = 4(1.5) + 1.2 = 7.2$ This one is also correct. $x = 3.25$

$f(x) = 4x + 1\frac{1}{5} = 4(3.25) + 1.2 = 14.2$ This one works too!

D. $f(x) = 5x + \frac{3}{10} = 5(0.5) + \frac{3}{10} = 2.8 \neq 3.2$

25) Answer: B

The diameter of a circle is twice the radius. Radius of the circle is $\frac{11}{2}$.

Area of a circle $= \pi r^2 = \pi(\frac{11}{2})^2 = 60.5\pi = 42.25 \times 3.14 = 189.97 \cong 190$

26) Answer: B

$$\text{Average (mean)} = \frac{sum\ of\ terms}{number\ of\ terms} = \frac{11+14+17+12+17+20+13.5}{7} = 14.93$$

27) Answer: B

Since, E is the midpoint of AB, then the area of all triangles DAE, DEF, CFE and CBE are equal.

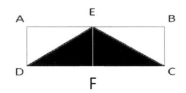

Let x be the area of one of the triangles, then: $4x = 160 \rightarrow x = 40$

The area of DEC $= 2x = 2(40) = 80$

28) Answer: C

A. Number of books sold in April is: 210

Number of books sold in July is: 330 $\rightarrow \frac{210}{330} = \frac{21}{33} \neq 3$

B. Number of books sold in July is: 330

Half the number of books sold in May is: $\frac{600}{3} = 200 \rightarrow 330 > 200$

C. Number of books sold in June is: 120

Half the number of books sold in April is: $\frac{210}{2} = 105 \rightarrow 120 > 105$ (it's correct)

D. $210 + 120 = 330 > 600$

29) Answer: B

α and β are complementary angles. The sum of complementary angles is 180 degrees.

$\alpha + \beta = 180° \rightarrow \beta = 180° - \alpha = 180° - 50° = 130°$

Then, $\frac{\alpha}{\beta} = \frac{50}{130} = \frac{5}{13}$

30) Answer: A

Prime factorizing of $63 = 3 \times 3 \times 7$

Prime factorizing of $21 = 3 \times 7$

LCM= $3 \times 3 \times 7 = 63$

Practice Test 5

FSA - Mathematics

Answers and Explanations

1) Answer: D

Plugin the value of x in the equations. $x = -2$, then:

A. $x(5x - 4) = 30 \rightarrow -2(5(-2) - 4) = -2(-10 - 4) = -2(-14) = 28 \neq 30$

B. $3(10 - x^2) = -16 \rightarrow 3(10 - (-2)^2) = 3(10 - 4) = 3(6) = 18 \neq -16$

C. $3(-3x + 5) = 30 \rightarrow 3(-3(-2) + 5) = 3(6 + 5) = 3(11) = 33 \neq 30$

D. $2x(-5x - 15) = 20 \rightarrow -4(-5(-2) - 15) = -4(-5) = 20 = 20$

2) Answer: D

Use Pythagorean theorem to find the hypotenuse of the triangle.

$a^2 + b^2 = c^2 \rightarrow 6^2 + 8^2 = c^2 \rightarrow 36 + 64 = c^2 \rightarrow 100 = c^2 \rightarrow c = 10$

The perimeter of the triangle is: $6 + 8 + 10 = 24$

3) Answer: D

Use percent formula:

$\text{Part} = \dfrac{\text{percent}}{100} \times \text{whole}$

$70 = \dfrac{\text{percent}}{100} \times 40 \Rightarrow 70 = \dfrac{\text{percent} \times 40}{100} \Rightarrow$

$70 = \dfrac{\text{percent} \times 2}{5}$, multiply both sides by 5.

$350 = \text{percent} \times 2$, divide both sides by 2.

$175 = \text{percent}$; The answer is 175%

4) Answer: C

Let's check the options provided.

A. $-6 + (-21 \div 7) + \dfrac{-8}{3} \times 3 \rightarrow -6 + (-3) + (-8) = -17$

B. $3 \times (-11) + (-4) \times 5 = (-33) + (-20) = -53$

C. $(-3) + 12 \times 5 \div (-4) = -3 + 60 \div (-4) = -3 - 15 = -18$

D. $(-3) \times (-7) + 3 = 21 + 3 = 24$

5) Answer: A

1 feet $= 12$ inches. Then: 540 in $\times \frac{1 \text{ ft}}{12 \text{ in}} = \frac{540}{12}$ ft $= 45$ ft

6) Answer: C

A. $0.09 = \frac{9}{100}$

B. $\frac{45}{100} = \frac{9}{20} = 0.45$

C. $5.3 = 5\frac{3}{10} = \frac{53}{10}$

D. $\frac{42}{7} = 6$

7) Answer: A

Prime factorizing of $15 = 3 \times 5$

Prime factorizing of $60 = 2 \times 2 \times 3 \times 5$

To find Greatest Common Factor, multiply the common factors of both numbers.

GCF$= 3 \times 5 = 15$

8) Answer: A

$-16 < -9 < -4 < 4 < 18 < 20$; Then choice A

9) Answer: B

Plug in the values of x in the equations provided.

A. $f(x) = 2x - \frac{3}{10} = 2(3.1) - \frac{3}{10} = 6.2 - 0.3 = 5.9 \neq 3.4$

B. $f(x) = x + \frac{3}{10} = 3.1 + \frac{3}{10} = 3.1 + 0.3 = 3.4$

C. $f(x) = 2x + 2\frac{2}{5} = 2(3.1) + \frac{12}{5} = 6.2 + 2.4 = 8.6 \neq 3.4$

D. $f(x) = 2x + \frac{3}{10} = 2(3.1) + 0.3 = 6.2 + 0.3 = 6.5 \neq 3.4$

10) Answer: B

Choices A, C and D are incorrect because 60% of each of the numbers is a non-whole number.

A. $64,$ $60\% \text{ of } 64 = 0.60 \times 64 = 38.4$

B. $25,$ $60\% \text{ of } 25 = 0.60 \times 25 = 15$

C. $46,$ $60\% \text{ of } 46 = 0.60 \times 46 = 27.6$

D. 52, $60\%\ of\ 52 = 0.60 \times 52 = 31.2$

11) Answer: D

First, we need to find the GCF (Greatest Common Factor) of 204 and 84.

$204 = 2 \times 2 \times 3 \times 17$

$84 = 2 \times 2 \times 3 \times 7 \rightarrow$ GCF $= 2 \times 2 \times 3 = 12$; Therefore, we need 12 boxes.

12) Answer: D

Distance that car B travels $= 3.5 \times$ distance that car A travels

$= 3.5 \times 243.26 = 851.41$ Km

13) Answer: D

A. $5^4 - 7^3 = 625 - 343 = 282$

B. $8^3 - 3^5 = 512 - 243 = 269$

C. $6^4 - 4^5 = 1,296 - 1,024 = 272$

D. $9^3 - 13^2 = 729 - 169 = 560$

14) Answer: C

The radius of the circle is: $\dfrac{5\pi}{2}$

The area of circle: $\pi r^2 = \pi(\dfrac{5\pi}{2})^2 = \pi \times \dfrac{25\pi^2}{4} = \dfrac{25\pi^3}{4}$

15) Answer: D

Elise has x apple which is 25 apples more than number of apples Alvin owns.

Therefore: $x - 25 = 55 \rightarrow x = 55 + 25 = 80$

Elise has 80 apples.

Let y be the number of apples that Baron has. Then: $y = \dfrac{1}{4} \times 80 = 20$

16) Answer: B

Let x and y be two sides of the shape. Then:

$x + 2 = 2 + 2 + 2 \rightarrow x = 4$

$y + 12 + 4 = 14 + 8 \rightarrow y + 16 = 22 \rightarrow y = 6$

Then, the perimeter is:

$2 + 14 + 2 + 8 + 2 + 4 + 2 + 12 + 4 + 6 = 56$

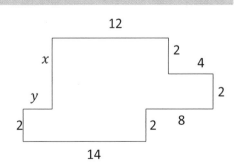

17) Answer: B

Complementary angles add up to 180 degrees.

$\beta + 140° = 180° \rightarrow \beta = 180° - 140° = 40°$

The sum of all angles in a triangle is 180 degrees. Then:

$\alpha + \beta + 70° = 180° \rightarrow \alpha + 40° + 70° = 180°$

$\rightarrow \alpha + 110° = 180° \rightarrow \alpha = 180° - 110° = 70°$

18) Answer: D

Two months, March and May, in 12 months start with M, then:

$\text{Probability} = \dfrac{number\ of\ desired\ outcomes}{number\ of\ total\ outcomes} = \dfrac{2}{12} = \dfrac{1}{6}$

19) Answer: B

$6(2.342) - 10.924 = 14.052 - 10.924 = 3.128$

20) Answer: B

The perimeter of the trapezoid is 53.

Therefore, the missing side (height) is $= 53 - 10 - 13 - 16 = 14$

Area of the trapezoid: $A = \dfrac{1}{2}h(b1 + b2) = \dfrac{1}{2}(14)\,(10 + 13) = 161$

21) Answer: D

First, put the numbers in order from least to greatest: 2, 2, 2, 3, 3, 4, 4, 5, 5, 6, 7

The Mode of the set of numbers is: 2 (the most frequent numbers)

Median is: 4 (the number in the middle)

22) Answer: B

The ratio of pens to pencils is 4: 6. Therefore there are 4 pens out of all 10 pens and

pencils. To find the answer, first dived 180 by 10 then multiply the result by 4.

$180 \div 10 = 18 \rightarrow 18 \times 4 = 72$

There are 72 pens and 108 pencils (180–72) Therefore, 36 more pens should be put in

the box to make the ratio 1: 1

23) Answer: C

$\dfrac{45}{8} = 5.63 \qquad \dfrac{5}{2} = 2.5 \qquad \dfrac{8}{15} \cong 0.533 \qquad \dfrac{9}{3} = 3$

Then: $\frac{8}{15} < \frac{5}{2} < \frac{9}{3} < \frac{45}{8}$

24) Answer: B

$5x - 4 = 16 \rightarrow 5x = 16 + 4 = 20 \rightarrow x = \frac{20}{5} = 4$

Then, $4x + 5 = 4(4) + 5 = 16 + 5 = 21$

25) Answer: A

Percent of cities in the type of pollution C: $\frac{5}{10} \times 100 = 50\%$

Percent of cities in the type of pollution B: $\frac{2}{10} \times 100 = 20\%$

Percent of cities in the type of pollution E: $\frac{6}{10} \times 100 = 60\%$

26) Answer: D

The area of the floor is: 6 cm × 35 cm = 210 cm²

The number of tiles needed = 210 ÷ 7 = 30

27) Answer: B

The shaft rotates 420 times in 7 seconds. Then, the number of rotates in 13 second equals to: $\frac{420 \times 13}{7} = 780$

28) Answer: A

Let's write an inequality for each statement.

A. $\frac{x}{7} \geq 9$ (this is the same as the inequality provided)

B. $\frac{7}{x} < 9$

C. $\frac{9}{x} = 7$

D. $\frac{x}{7} > 9$

29) Answer: A

Check each option provided:

A. 5 $\frac{2+6+8+10+11}{5} = \frac{37}{5} = 7.4$

B. 6 $\frac{2+5+8+10+11}{5} = \frac{36}{5} = 7.2$

C. 2 $\qquad \frac{5+6+8+10+11}{5} = \frac{40}{5} = 8$

D. 10 $\qquad \frac{2+5+6+8+11}{5} = \frac{32}{5} = 6.4$

30) Answer: D

If the value of point A is greater than the value of point B, then the distance of two points on the number line is: value of A− value of B

A. $-\frac{15}{3} - (-13) = -5 + 13 = 8 = 8$

B. $3 - \left(-\frac{15}{3}\right) = 3 + 5 = 8 = 8$

C. $-2 - \left(-\frac{15}{3}\right) = -2 + 5 = 3 \neq 8$

Practice Test 6

FSA - Mathematics

Answers and Explanations

1) Answer: A

For one hour he earns \$20, then for t hours he earns \$20t. If he wants to earn at least \$350, therefor, the number of working hours multiplied by 20 must be equal to 350 or more than 350.

$$20t \geq 350$$

2) Answer: C

Plug in the value of x and y and use order of operations rule.

$x = 2$ and $y = -1$

$3(2x - 3y) + (1 - 3x)^2 = 3(2(2) - 3(-1)) + (1 - 3(2))^2 = 3(4 + 3) + (-5)^2 =$
$21 + 25 = 46$

3) Answer: C

$$\frac{565}{9} \cong 62.77 \cong 62.8$$

4) Answer: C

Opposite number of any number x is a number that if added to x, the result is 0. Then:

$19 + (-19) = 0$ and $0 + 0 = 0$

5) Answer: A

The coordinate plane has two axes. The vertical line is called the y-axis and the horizontal is called the x-axis. The points on the coordinate plane are address using the form (x, y). The point A is one unit on the left side of x-axis; therefore, its x value is 1 and it is three units down, therefore its y axis is -3. The coordinate of the point is: $(1, -3)$

6) Answer: A

$72: 12 = 18: 3$

$18 \times 4 = 72$ And $3 \times 4 = 12$

7) Answer: C

$(86 + 14) \div (20) = (100) \div (20)$

The prime factorization of 100 is: $2 \times 2 \times 5 \times 5$

The prime factorization of 20 is: 4×5

Therefore: $(100) \div (20) = (2 \times 2 \times 5 \times 5) \div (4 \times 5)$

8) Answer: A

Solve for x.

$-6 \le 2x - 8 < -4 \Rightarrow$ (add 8 all sides) $-6 + 8 \le 2x - 8 + 8 < -4 + 8 \Rightarrow$

$2 \le 2x < 4 \Rightarrow$ (divide all sides by 2) $1 \le x < 2$

x is between 1 and 2. Choice A represent this inequality.

9) Answer: D

The ratio of boy to girls is 4:6. Therefore, there are 4 boys out of 10 students. To find the answer, first divide the total number of students by 10, then multiply the result by 4.

$500 \div 10 = 50 \Rightarrow 50 \times 4 = 200$

10) Answer: D

Volume of a box = length × width × height = $9 \times 7 \times 4 = 252$

11) Answer: B

$\text{Probability} = \dfrac{number\ of\ desired\ outcomes}{number\ of\ total\ outcomes} = \dfrac{20}{18+20+16+14} = \dfrac{20}{68} = \dfrac{5}{17}$

12) Answer: D

All the statements are true.

13) Answer: C

Let's compare each fraction: $\dfrac{3}{5} < \dfrac{5}{7} < \dfrac{27}{30} < \dfrac{13}{6}$

Only choice C provides the right order.

14) Answer: B

$4 \times \dfrac{7}{9} = \dfrac{28}{9} = 3.11$

A. $3.11 > 3$

B. $3.11 > 3$ This is the answer!

C. $\frac{81}{37} = 2.2 \neq 3.11$

D. $2.5 < 3.11$

15) Answer: B

The slope of the line is: $\frac{y_2 - y_1}{x_2 - x_1} = \frac{8-3}{3-2} = \frac{5}{1} = 5$

The equation of a line can be written as:

$y - y_0 = m(x - x_0) \rightarrow y - 3 = 5(x - 2) \rightarrow y - 3 = 5x - 10 \rightarrow y = 5x - 7$

16) Answer: A

1 yard = 3 feet

Therefore, 3,756 ft.$\times \frac{1\,yd}{3\,ft} = 1{,}252$ yd

17) Answer: C

Simplify each option provided.

A. $-20 - (4 \times 11) + (8 \times 25) = -20 - 44 + 200 = 136$

B. $\left(\frac{13}{9} \times 99\right) + \left(\frac{156}{2}\right) = 143 + 78 = 221$

C. $\left(\left(\frac{19}{4} + \frac{35}{4}\right) \times 9\right) - \frac{25}{2} + \frac{164}{4} = \left(\left(\frac{19+35}{4}\right) \times 9\right) - \frac{25}{2} + \frac{164}{4} = \left(\left(\frac{27}{2}\right) \times 9\right) + \frac{164-50}{4} =$

$\frac{243}{2} + \frac{57}{2} = \frac{300}{2} = 150$ (this is the answer)

D. $\frac{278}{6} + \frac{221}{3} + 50 = \frac{278+442}{6} + 50 = 120 + 50 = 170$

18) Answer: C

3,800 out of 49,400 equals to $\frac{3{,}800}{49{,}400} = \frac{1}{13}$

19) Answer: B

The area of the trapezoid is: $area = \frac{(base\ 1 + base\ 2)}{2} \times height = \left(\frac{11+15}{2}\right)x = A \rightarrow$

$13x = A \rightarrow x = \frac{A}{13}$

20) Answer: B

To find the discount, multiply the number $(100\% - \text{rate of discount})$

Therefore; $900(100\% - 30\%) = 900(1 - 0.3) = 900 - (900 \times 0.3)$

21) Answer: C

When points are reflected over y-axis, the value of y in the coordinates doesn't change and the sign of x changes. Therefore, the coordinates of point B is $(8, 9)$.

22) Answer: C

There are 30 integers from 1 to 30. Set of numbers that are not composite between 1 and 30 is: A= {1, 2, 3, 5, 7, 11, 13, 17, 19, 23, 29}

11 integers are not composite. Probability of not selecting a composite number is:

$$\text{Probability} = \frac{number\ of\ desired\ outcomes}{number\ of\ total\ outcomes} = \frac{11}{30}$$

23) Answer: A

$\frac{256}{16} = 16, \frac{4,096}{256} = 16, \frac{65,536}{4,096} = 16$; Therefore, the factor is 16

24) Answer: C

Plug in the value of x into the function $f(x)$. First, plug in 2.2 for x.

A. $f(x) = 2x - \frac{2}{5} = 2(2.2) - \frac{2}{5} = 4 \neq 9.8$

B. $f(x) = x + \frac{2}{5} = 2.2 + \frac{2}{5} = 2.6 \neq 9.8$

C. $f(x) = 3x + 3\frac{1}{5} = 3(2.2) + 3\frac{1}{5} = 6.6 + 3.2 = 9.8$ This is correct!

Plug in other values of x. $x = 3.6$

$f(x) = 3x + 3\frac{1}{5} = 3(3.6) + 3.2 = 14$ This one is also correct. $x = 5.1$

$f(x) = 3x + 3\frac{1}{5} = 3(5.1) + 3.2 = 18.5$ This one works too!

D. $4x + \frac{4}{10} = 4(2.2) + \frac{4}{10} = 9.2 \neq 9.8$

25) Answer: B

The diameter of a circle is twice the radius. Radius of the circle is $\frac{13}{2}$.

Area of a circle $= \pi r^2 = \pi(\frac{13}{2})^2 = 42.25\pi = 42.25 \times 3.14 = 132.665 \cong 133$

26) Answer: B

$$\text{Average (mean)} = \frac{sum\ of\ terms}{number\ of\ terms} = \frac{10+13+16+11+16+18+14.5}{7} = 14.07$$

27) Answer: B

Since, E is the midpoint of AB, then the area of all triangles DAE, DEF, CFE and CBE are equal.

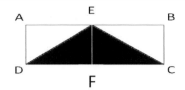

Let x be the area of one of the triangles, then: $4x = 120 \rightarrow x = 30$

The area of DEC $= 2x = 2(30) = 60$

28) Answer: C

A. Number of books sold in April is: 980

Number of books sold in July is: $1,560 \rightarrow \frac{980}{1,560} = \frac{49}{78} \neq 2$

B. Number of books sold in July is: 1,560

Half the number of books sold in May is $\frac{2,500}{2} = 1,250 \rightarrow 1,560 > 1,250$

C. Number of books sold in June is: 600

Half the number of books sold in April is: $\frac{980}{2} = 490 \rightarrow 600 > 490$ (it's correct)

D. $980 + 600 = 1,580 > 1,560$

29) Answer: B

α and β are complementary angles. The sum of complementary angles is 180 degrees.

$\alpha + \beta = 180° \rightarrow \beta = 180° - \alpha = 180° - 80° = 100°$

Then, $\frac{\alpha}{\beta} = \frac{80}{100} = \frac{8}{10} = \frac{4}{5}$

30) Answer: A

Prime factorizing of $45 = 3 \times 3 \times 5$

Prime factorizing of $15 = 3 \times 5$

LCM$= 3 \times 3 \times 5 = 45$

"End"

Made in the USA
Columbia, SC
28 April 2022

59617033R00076